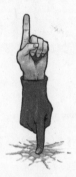

Volume 11. Published in the 11th month, containing
the #1 hero's climactic battle. Lots of ones.

**KOHEI HORIKOSHI**

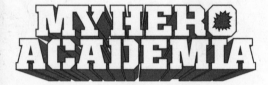

## 11

### SHONEN JUMP Manga Edition

## STORY & ART KOHEI HORIKOSHI

TRANSLATION & ENGLISH ADAPTATION **Caleb Cook**
TOUCH-UP ART & LETTERING **John Hunt**
DESIGNER **Julian [JR] Robinson**
SHONEN JUMP SERIES EDITOR **John Bae**
GRAPHIC NOVEL EDITOR **Mike Montesa**

BOKU NO HERO ACADEMIA © 2014 by Kohei Horikoshi
All rights reserved.
First published in Japan in 2014 by SHUEISHA Inc., Tokyo.
English translation rights arranged by SHUEISHA Inc.

The stories, characters and incidents mentioned in this publication are entirely fictional.

Printed in the U.S.A.

Published by VIZ Media, LLC
P.O. Box 77010
San Francisco, CA 94107

10 9 8 7 6 5 4 3 2 1
First printing, February 2018

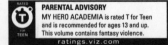

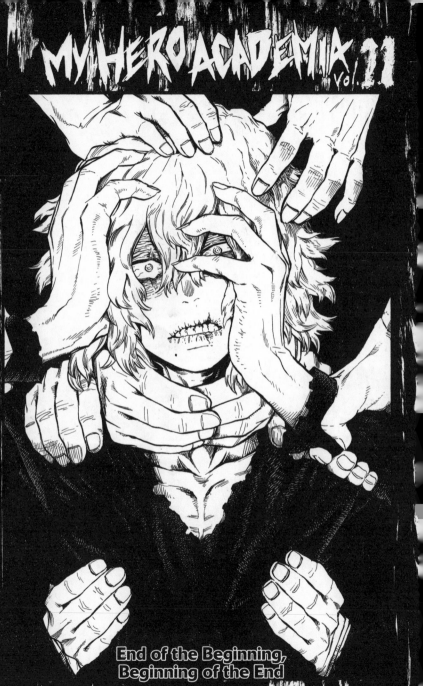

# MY HERO ACADEMIA Vol. 11

**End of the Beginning, Beginning of the End**

KOHEI HORIKOSHI

SHONEN JUMP MANGA

ALL MIGHT
IZUKU MIDORIYA
KATSUKI BAKUGO
SHOTO TODOROKI

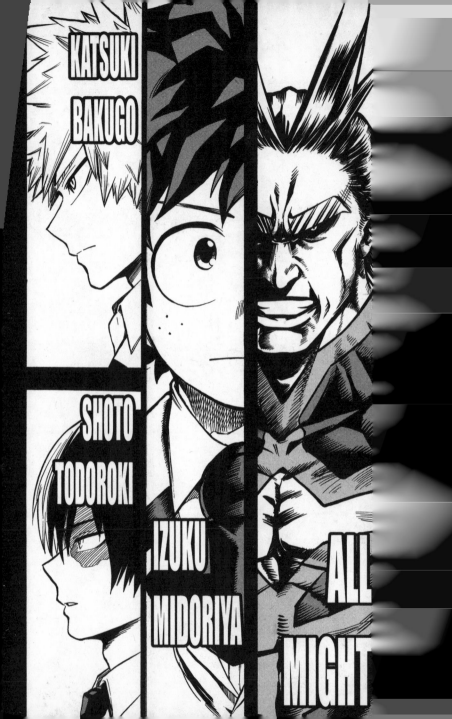

One day, people began manifesting special abilities that came to be known as "Quirks," and before long, the world was full of superpowered humans. But with the advent of these exceptional individuals came an increase in crime, and governments alone were unable to deal with the situation. At the same time, others emerged to oppose the spread of evil! As if straight from the comic books, these heroes keep the peace and are even officially authorized to fight crime. Our story begins when a certain Quirkless boy and lifelong hero fan meets the world's number one hero, starting him on his path to becoming the greatest hero ever!

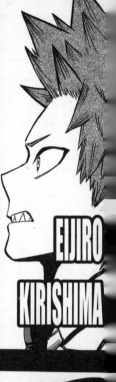

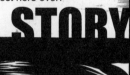

# STORY


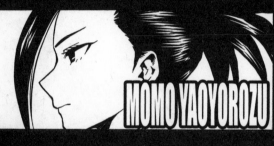

EIJIRO KIRISHIMA
MOMO YAOYOROZU
TENYA IDA
TOMURA SHIGARAKI
ALL FOR ONE

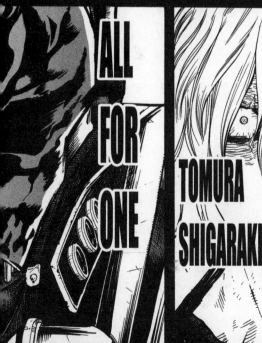

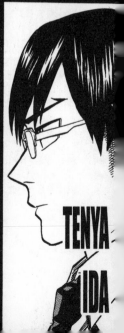

# MY HERO ACADEMIA

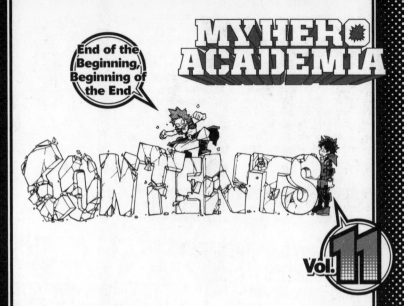

## End of the Beginning, Beginning of the End



# CONTENTS

Vol. 11

WHAM
WHAT TOOK YOU SO LONG?
No. 90 - Reach Out

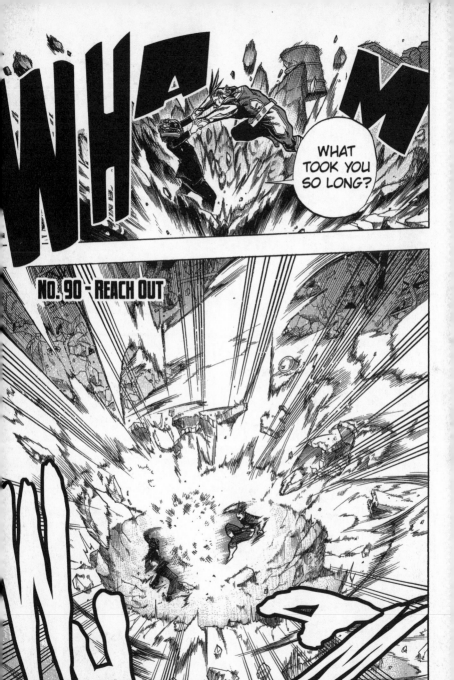

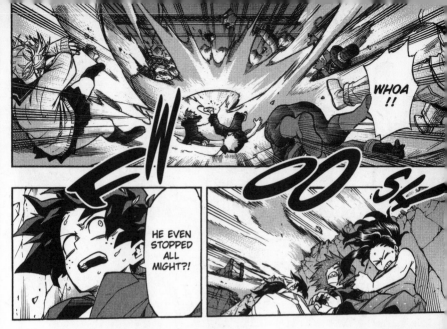

WHOA!!
GWOOSH
HE EVEN STOPPED ALL MIGHT?!
IT'S ABOUT FIVE KILOMETERS FROM THE BAR TO HERE...
AND IT TOOK YOU A WHOLE 30 SECONDS TO ARRIVE AFTER I SENT THE NOMU...
YOU'RE LOSING IT, ALL MIGHT.
SO ARE YOU.
WHAT'S WITH THAT INDUSTRIAL-LOOKING MASK?!
ARE YOU SURE YOU SHOULD BE UP AND ABOUT IN THAT STATE?!

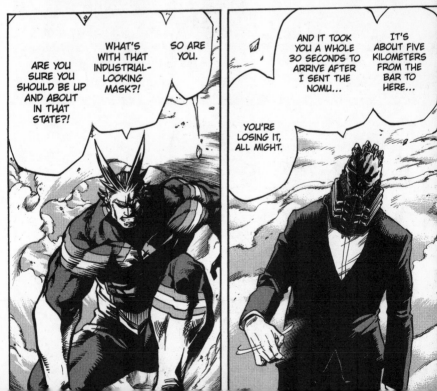

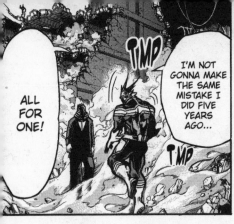

HE BLOCKED ALL MIGHT'S PUNCH WITH HIS BARE HANDS!
HE'S GOTTA BE THE VILLAINS' BOSS!
TMP
I'M NOT GONNA MAKE THE SAME MISTAKE I DID FIVE YEARS AGO...
ALL FOR ONE!
TMP
I'M TAKING BAKUGO!
AND THIS TIME, I'M SMASHING YOU INTO A PRISON CELL!
YOU AND YOUR LITTLE LEAGUE OF VILLAINS!!
DASH
SOUNDS LIKE...
...THERE'S A LOT ON YOUR TO-DO LIST.
FWIP
YOU AND ME BOTH.
GWO
OOM

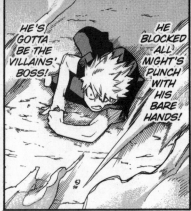

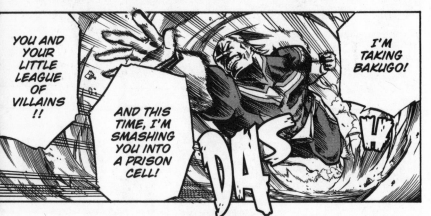

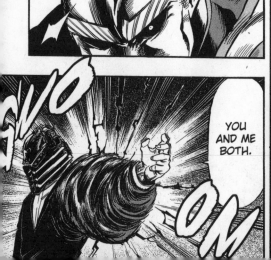

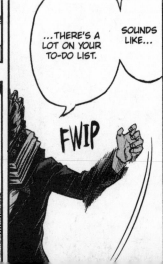

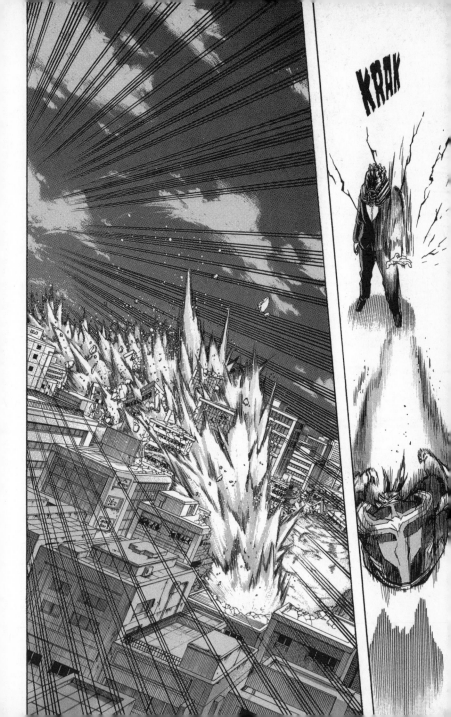

KRAK

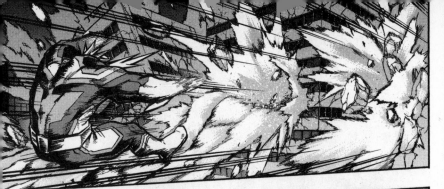

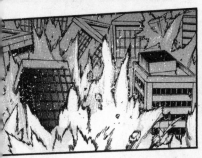

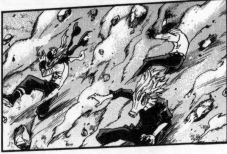

THAT'S AN AIR CANNON ...
...PLUS SPRINGLIKE LIMBS, KINETICALLY BOOSTED BY FOUR AND THE STRENGTH ENHANCED BY THREE.
IT'S A FUN LITTLE COMBINATION... BUT I WANT TO ADD IN A FEW MORE POWER-UP-TYPE QUIRKS...
ALL MIGHT !!
DON'T FRET. THAT WON'T BE ENOUGH TO KILL HIM.
SO...

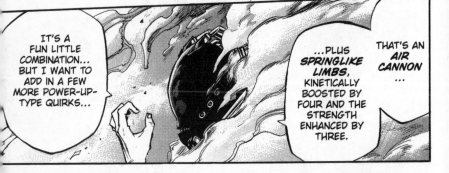

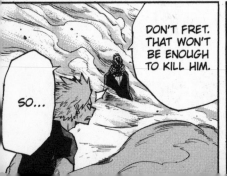

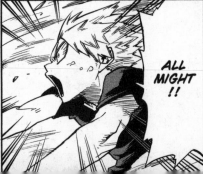

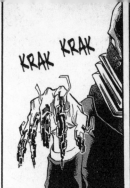

YOU NEED TO FLEE, TOMURA.
FWIP
AND TAKE THE BOY WITH YOU.
KRAK KRAK
KUROGIRI WILL HELP WITH YOUR ESCAPE.
SHUNK
SHUNK
SHUNK
HEY, YOU! THE POOR FELLOW'S BEEN KNOCKED UNCONSCIOUS!!
I'M NOT SURE HOW YOU DO IT, BUT COULDN'T YOU USE *YOUR* WARP ABILITY TO HELP US GET AWAY?
TWITCH
TWITCH
MY VERSION'S STILL NOT ***COMPLETE***, MAGNE. IT ONLY WORKS OVER EXTREMELY SHORT DISTANCES, AND...
...IT'S NOT LIKE HIS, WHICH CAN TARGET SPECIFIC COORDINATES. ALL I CAN DO IS BRING THINGS *TO* ME OR SEND THEM *AWAY* FROM ME.
WHRR
WHAT'S MORE... THE DESTINATION HAS TO BE A ***PERSON***... ONE I'M WELL ACQUAINTED WITH.
WHRR
WHRR

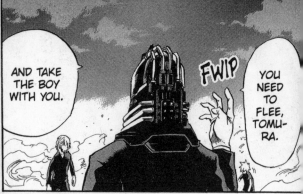

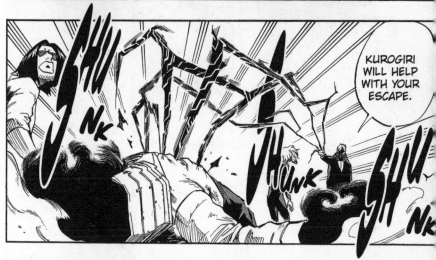

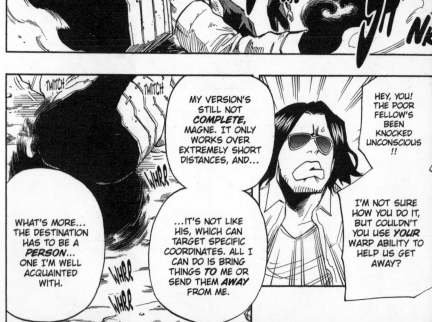

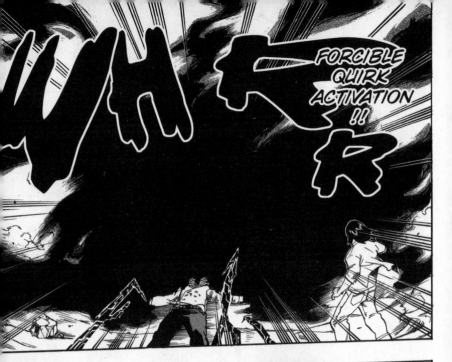

FORCIBLE
QUIRK
ACTIVATION
!!

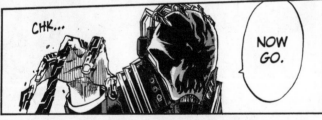

CHK...

NOW
GO.

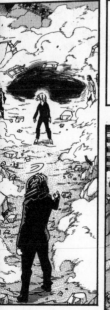

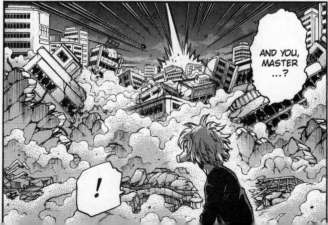

AND YOU,
MASTER
...?

!

YOU WON'T GET AWAY !!
ALWAYS THINK AHEAD, TOMURA.
YOU STILL HAVE MUCH ROOM TO GROW.
TMP

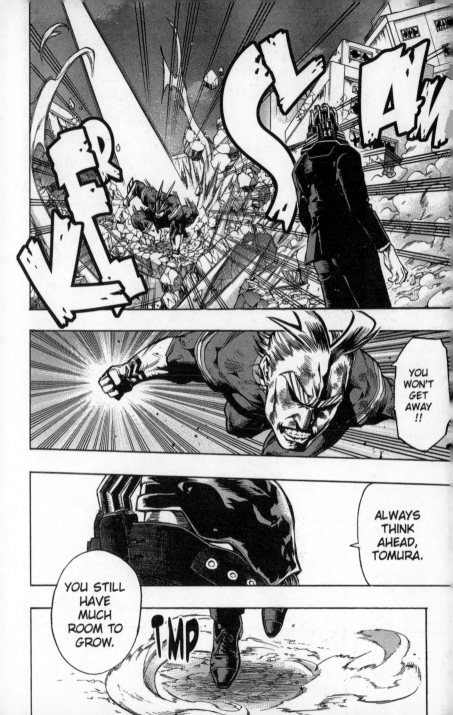

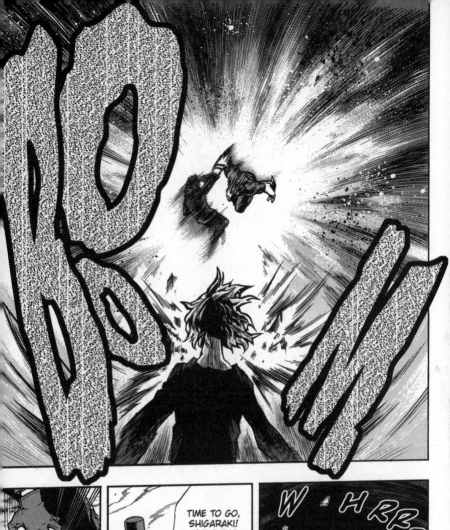

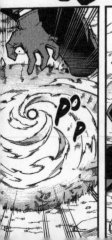

POP P

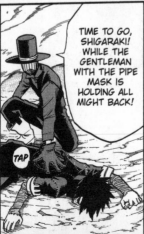

TIME TO GO, SHIGARAKI! WHILE THE GENTLEMAN WITH THE PIPE MASK IS HOLDING ALL MIGHT BACK!

TAP

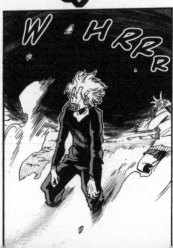

W HRRR

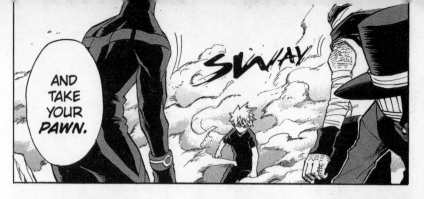

SWAY
AND TAKE YOUR PAWN.
WHAT A PAIN...
BAKUGO, KID...!!
RRMBBBB
ALL MIGHT...!
HE'S HAVING TROUBLE RESCUING KACCHAN BECAUSE OF ALL FOR ONE!
AND THE LEAGUE'S TAKING THE OPPORTUNITY TO GRAB KACCHAN AND ESCAPE!

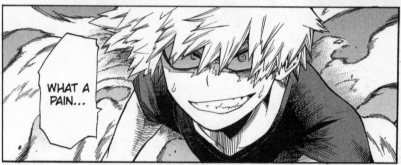

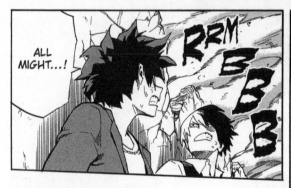

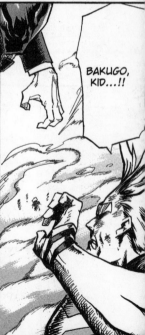

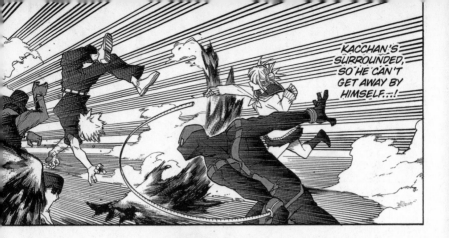

KACCHAN'S SURROUNDED, SO HE CAN'T GET AWAY BY HIMSELF...!
THESE GUYS HAVE ME ON THE ROPES.
IT'S NOT LIKE BEFORE. THEY'RE GONNA TRY TO TAKE ME BY FORCE.
AND IT'S SIX-ON-ONE...
BOOM
FIRST OFF, GOTTA KEEP THIS MASKED BASTARD FROM TOUCHING ME!
I'M COMING FOR YOU!!
FWIP

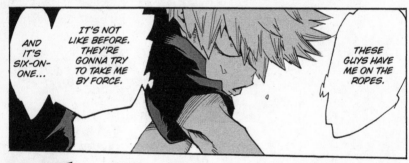

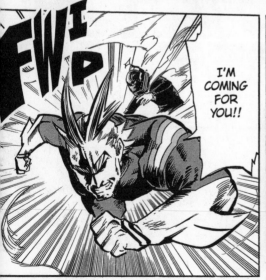

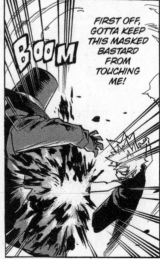

SLAM
NOT SO FAST.
THAT'S WHY *I'M* HERE.
GWOM
SKF
SKF
SKF
SKF
SKF
SKF
EVEN IN A PINCH LIKE THIS...!!
EVEN NOW...!!

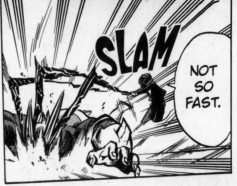

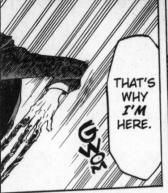

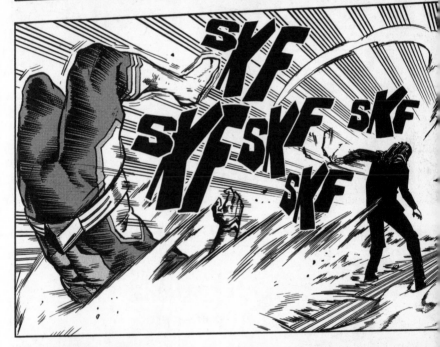

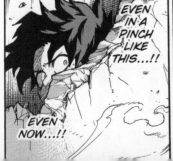

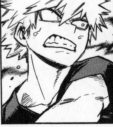

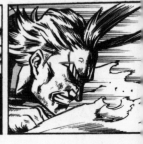

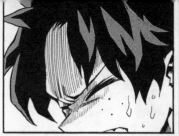

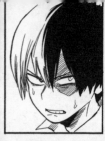

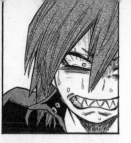

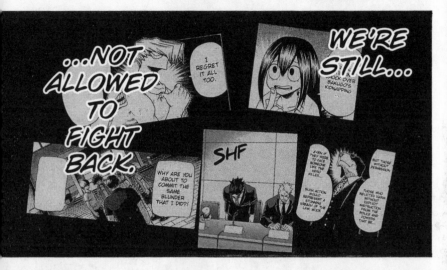

WE'RE STILL...
SHOCK OVER BAKUGO'S KIDNAPPING ...
...NOT ALLOWED TO FIGHT BACK.
I REGRET IT ALL TOO.
BUT THOSE WITHOUT PERMISSION ...
THOSE WHO INFLICTED HARM WITHOUT EXPLICIT INSTRUCTION FROM THE POLICE AND POWERS THAT BE...
EVEN IF THEY WERE TO FACE SOMEONE LIKE THE HERO KILLER...
SUCH ACTION WOULD REPRESENT A STUNNING BREACH OF THE LAW. WOOF.
SHF
WHY ARE YOU ABOUT TO COMMIT THE SAME BLUNDER THAT I DID?!
JUST NEED...AN OPENING...!! SOMEWHERE!! JUST FOR AN INSTANT.
THERE HAS TO BE A WAY TO RESCUE KACCHAN!
WITH KACCHAN OUT OF HARM'S WAY...
...ALL MIGHT CAN FIGHT WITHOUT HOLDING BACK!
ALL MIGHT...
...!

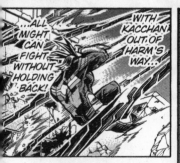

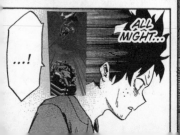

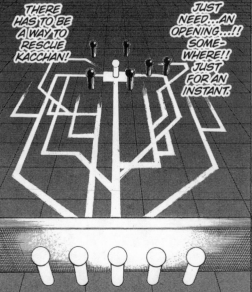

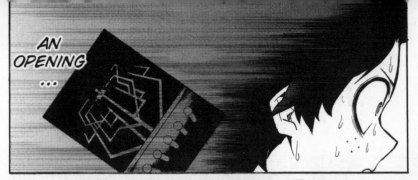

AN OPENING ...
IDA!
EVERYONE!
DON'T EVEN THINK ABOUT IT... MIDORIYA!
NO, THERE'S A WAY!
IT WON'T TECHNICALLY COUNT AS FIGHTING!
AND IT'LL HELP US GET AWAY FROM HERE!
PLUS, WE'LL BE SAVING KACCHAN AT THE SAME TIME!!
SPIT IT OUT ALREADY.
BUT...IT RELIES ON KACCHAN'S COOPERATION ...

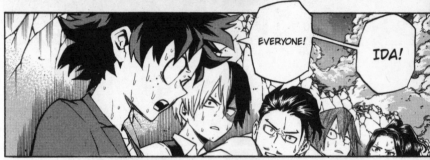

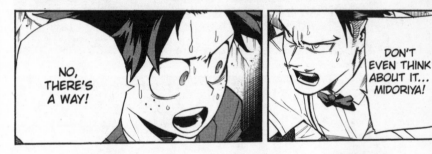

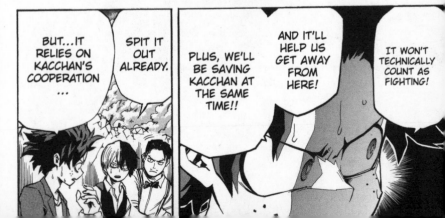

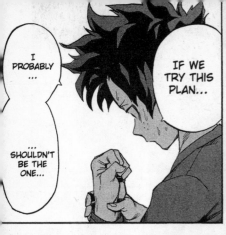

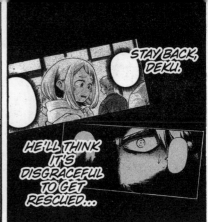

STAY BACK, DEKU.
HE'LL THINK IT'S DISGRACEFUL TO GET RESCUED...
IF WE TRY THIS PLAN...
I PROBABLY ...
... SHOULDN'T BE THE ONE...
IT HAS TO BE YOU, KIRISHIMA.
YOU'RE THE KEY TO OUR SUCCESS HERE.
BOOM...
KACCHAN IS ALWAYS WARY OF HIS OPPONENTS.
HE TRIES TO FIGHT FROM A DISTANCE.
WE'LL MOVE WHEN HE'S AT LEAST TWO STEPS AWAY FROM THE VILLAINS.
IDA...
THIS FEELS LIKE A GAMBLE, BUT CONSIDERING THE SITUATION, IT PUTS US AT LITTLE RISK.
AND SHOULD WE SUCCEED ...
...IT COULD CHANGE EVERY-THING...

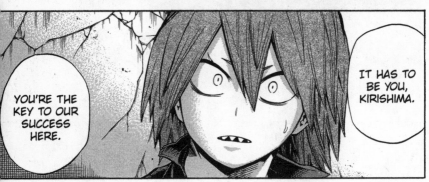

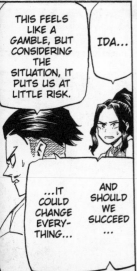

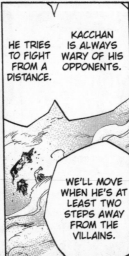

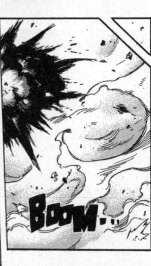

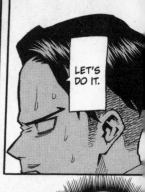

LET'S DO IT.
FIRST, WE USE MY FULL COWLING AND IDA'S RECIPRO TO GET US MOVING!
SHMP
CRASH!!
THE SECOND WE BREAK THROUGH, TODOROKI USES HIS ICE...
...TO CONSTRUCT A RAMP!
THEN, KIRISHIMA'S HARDENING WILL SMASH THROUGH THE WALL!
KRAKL
IT HAS TO BE TALL...
DRRRRR
...SO WE CAN REALLY FLY.

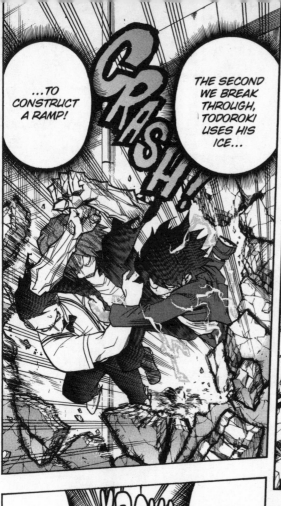

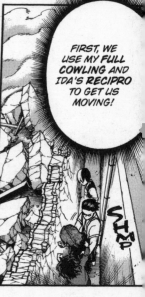

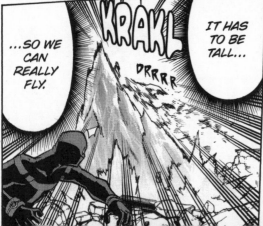

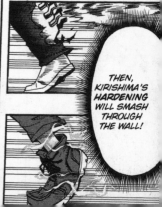

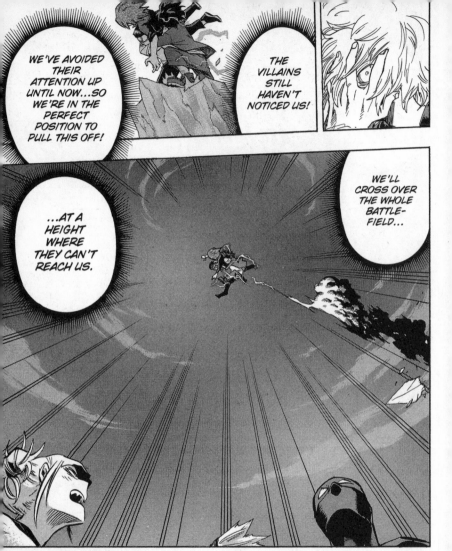

THE VILLAINS STILL HAVEN'T NOTICED US!
WE'VE AVOIDED THEIR ATTENTION UP UNTIL NOW...SO WE'RE IN THE PERFECT POSITION TO PULL THIS OFF!
WE'LL CROSS OVER THE WHOLE BATTLE-FIELD...
...AT A HEIGHT WHERE THEY CAN'T REACH US.
THE BOSS VILLAIN IS KEEPING ALL MIGHT PINNED DOWN.
WHICH MEANS...
HE'S ALSO NOT GOING ANY-WHERE!!

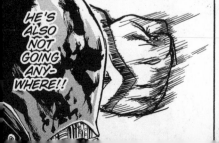

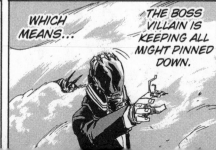

THEN...IT'S UP TO YOU, KIRISHIMA.
IT CAN'T BE ME.
IT CAN'T BE TODOROKI OR IDA OR YAOYOROZU EITHER...
EVER SINCE WE STARTED SCHOOL...
...YOU'VE BEEN BUILDING A RAPPORT WITH KACCHAN.
THIS HORSE WON'T BREAK!
YOU WANNA TAKE MIDORIYA DOWN, RIGHT?!
YOU'LL BE CALLING OUT TO HIM AS A FRIEND!!
COME ON!!

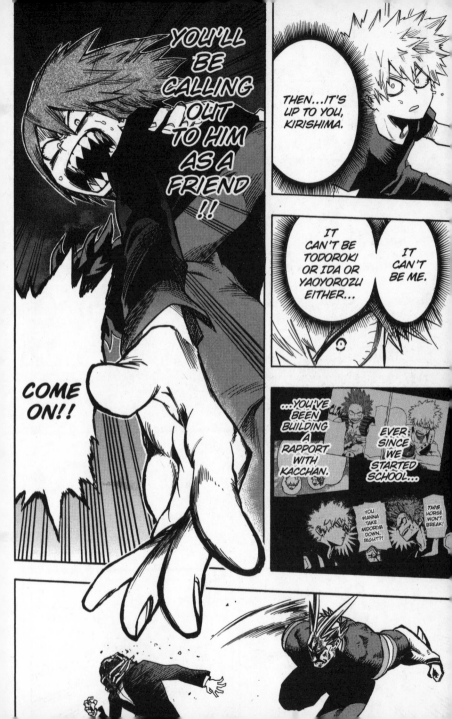

YOU IDIOTS...
GRAB

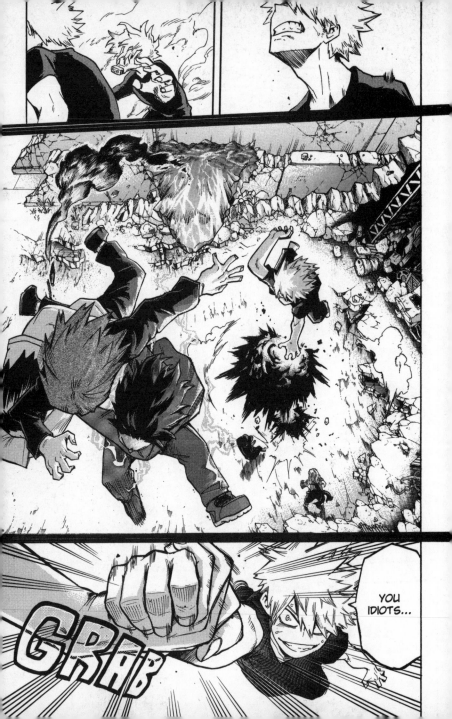

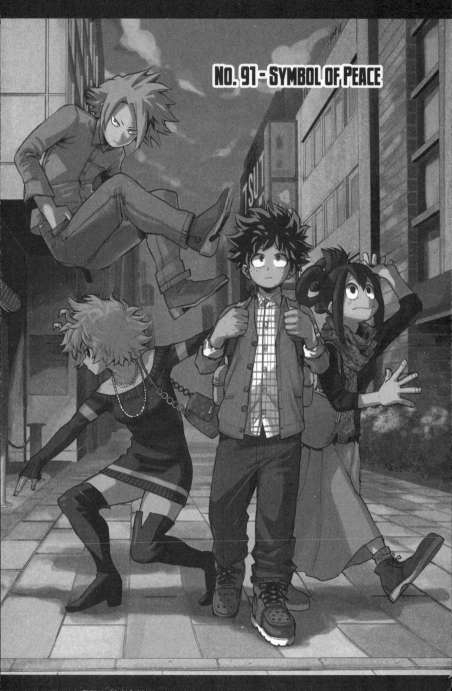

NO. 91 - SYMBOL OF PEACE

手前
da.co.jp
-2635

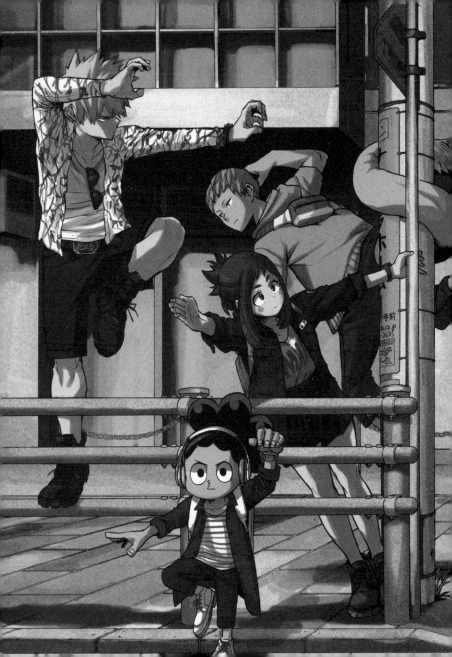

MY HERO ACADEMIA

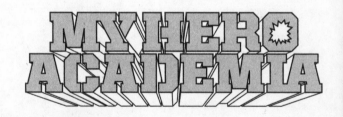

SEEING ALL MIGHT IN ACTION...
ALL MIGHT'S HAVING A TOUGH TIME FIGHTING...
...CUZ I'M IN THE WAY.
MY RECIPRO SHOULD HELP US GET AWAY! THEN ALL MIGHT CAN DO WHAT HE NEEDS TO...!!
I BET KACCHAN UNDERSTANDS WHAT WE HAFTA DO!
...SOMEHOW FREED US FROM THE FEAR THAT WAS HOLDING US BACK.

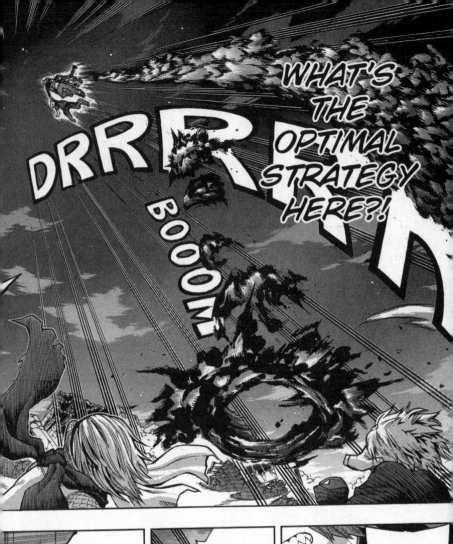

WHAT'S THE OPTIMAL STRATEGY HERE?!
DRRRR
BOOOOM
BAKUGO. WHEN I GIVE THE SIGNAL, TIME YOUR EXPLOSIONS IN SYNC WITH MY...
HOW ABOUT *YOU* SYNC UP WITH *ME*?
THIS IS NO TIME FOR EGOS!
JUST AS PLANNED! THE ENEMY'S STUNNED.
THIS IS OUR CHANCE TO RUN.

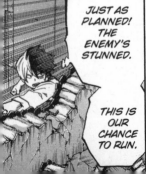

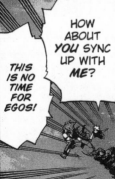

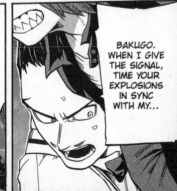

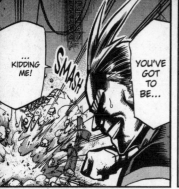

WHAAAAAT?!
WHERE ...
...DID THEY COME FROM?!
YOU'VE GOT TO BE...
SMASH
... KIDDING ME!
WE CAN'T LET THEM ESCAPE! WHO'S GOT A LONG-DISTANCE ATTACK?!
DABI AND KUROGIRI, BUT THEY'RE BOTH OUT!
YOU TWO, STICK TOGETHER!!
MAGNE QUIRK: MAGNETISM
HE CAN MAGNETIZE ANYONE WITHIN A 4.5-METER RADIUS OF HIMSELF!
HE CAN APPLY THE EFFECT TO A PERSON'S WHOLE BODY OR TO SPECIFIC BODY PARTS!
MEN BECOME "SOUTH POLES" AND WOMEN BECOME "NORTH POLES"!! HE CAN'T MAGNETIZE HIMSELF, THOUGH!
S
KZZZT
HERE WE GO!

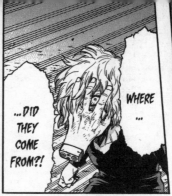

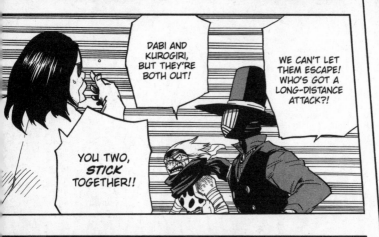

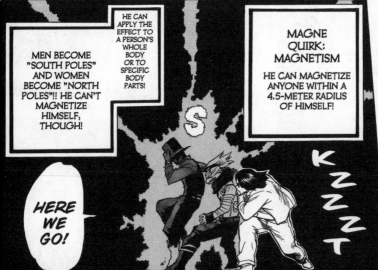

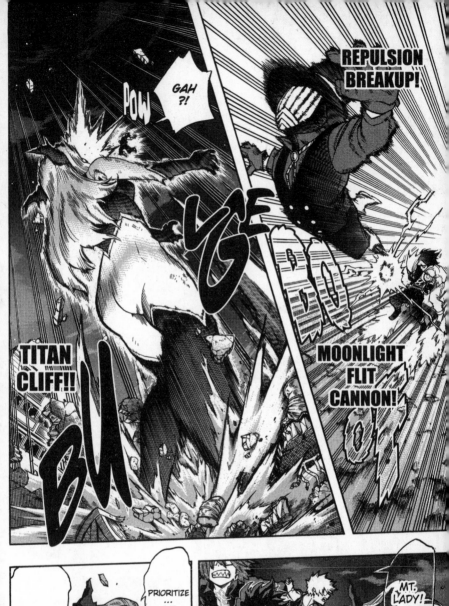

REPULSION BREAKUP!
MOONLIGHT FLIT CANNON!
POW
GAH ?!
TITAN CLIFF!!
MT. LADY!
PRIORITIZE ... THE RESCUE.
GO ON...! YOU DUMB KIDS...

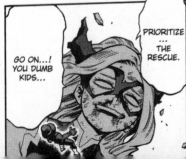

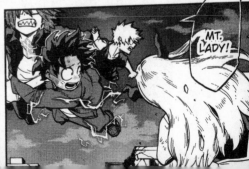

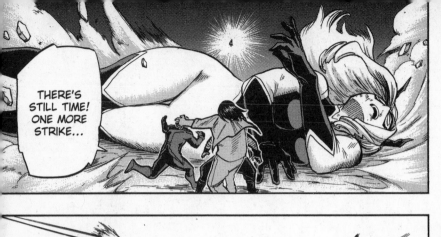

THERE'S STILL TIME! ONE MORE STRIKE...

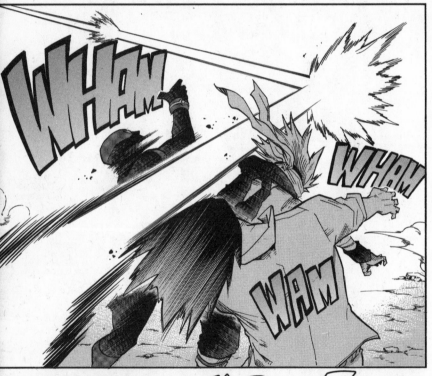

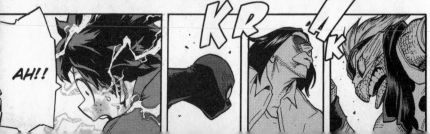

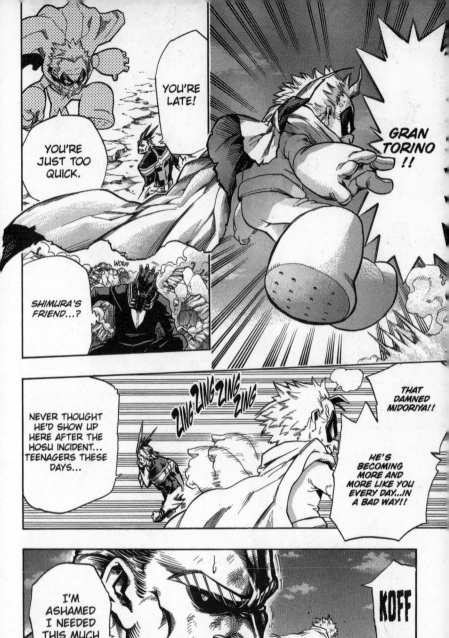

GRAN TORINO !!
YOU'RE LATE!
YOU'RE JUST TOO QUICK.
WORMP
SHIMURA'S FRIEND...?
THAT DAMNED MIDORIYA!!
HE'S BECOMING MORE AND MORE LIKE YOU EVERY DAY...IN A BAD WAY!!
ZING ZING ZING ZING
NEVER THOUGHT HE'D SHOW UP HERE AFTER THE HOSU INCIDENT... TEENAGERS THESE DAYS...
KOFF
I'M ASHAMED I NEEDED THIS MUCH HELP, BUT...

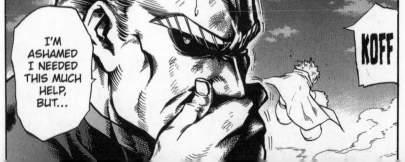

NOW THERE'S NO HOLDING BACK!
BAM
I'M GONNA...
...PUT YOU DOWN FOR GOOD!

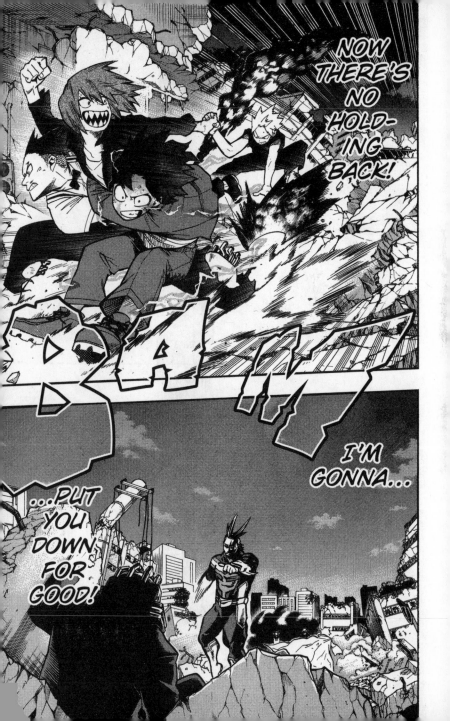

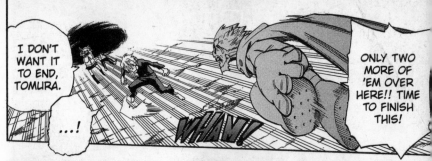

ONLY TWO MORE OF 'EM OVER HERE!! TIME TO FINISH THIS!
I DON'T WANT IT TO END, TOMURA.
WHAM!
...!
SHK
YOU GOT ME. YOU'VE SINGLE-HANDEDLY...
FWISH
... TURNED THE TABLES.
?!
SHK SHK
FORCED QUIRK ACTIVATION..
KZZZ
MAGNETISM!!

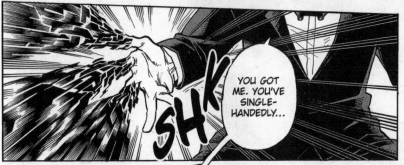

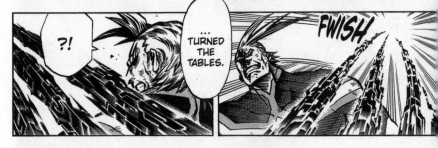

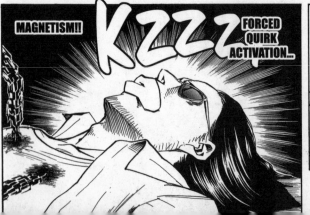

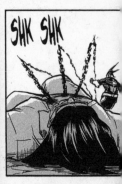

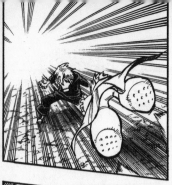

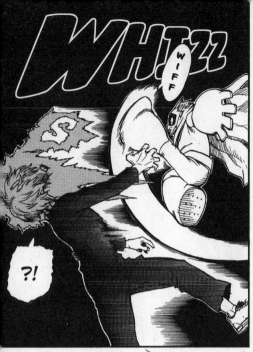

WHIZZ

WIFF

?!

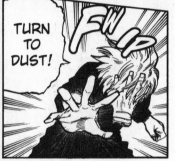

TURN
TO
DUST!

FWIP

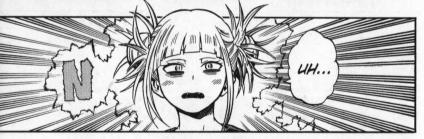

N

UH...

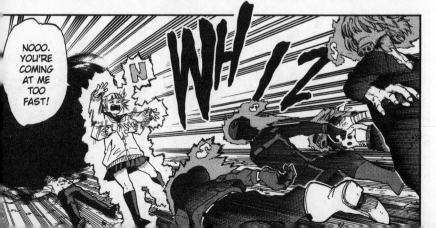

NOOO.
YOU'RE
COMING
AT ME
TOO
FAST!

N

WHIZ

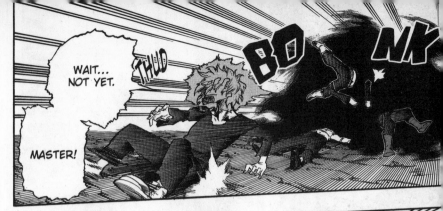

WAIT... NOT YET.

MASTER!

THUD

BO NK

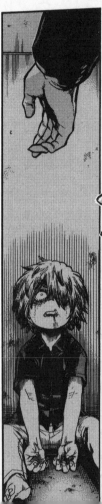

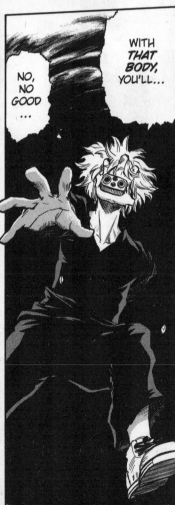

NO, NO GOOD ...

WITH *THAT BODY,* YOU'LL...

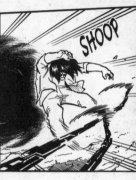

SHOOP

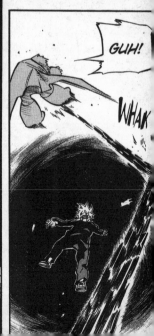

GUH!

WHAK

WHRR
I'M NOT READY...
FWOOSH
TOMURA.
YOU WILL CONTINUE THIS WAR.

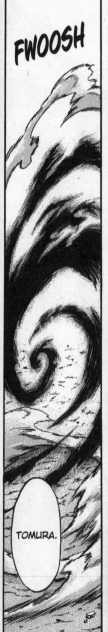

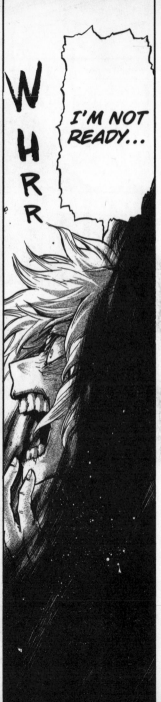

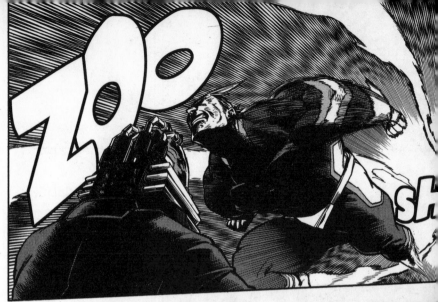

ZOO

SH

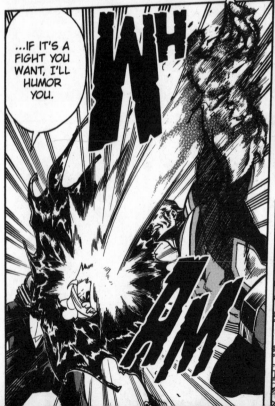

...IF IT'S A FIGHT YOU WANT, I'LL HUMOR YOU.

WHM

AM

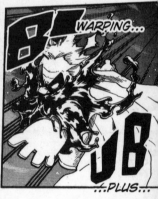

WARPING...

B

JB

...PLUS...

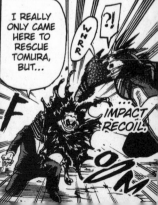

I REALLY ONLY CAME HERE TO RESCUE TOMURA, BUT...

WHRR

?!

F

...IMPACT RECOIL.

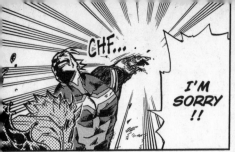

I'M SORRY!!
CHF...
BECAUSE ABOVE ALL, I DETEST YOU.
THERE WAS A TIME WHEN YOU WENT AROUND TAKING OUT MY ALLIES RIGHT AND LEFT WITH THOSE FISTS OF YOURS.
AND THEY CALLED YOU THE SYMBOL OF PEACE BECAUSE OF IT.
SWIP
YOU STOOD SO TALL ATOP ALL OF OUR SACRIFICES.
HOW WAS THE VIEW FROM UP THERE?
BOOM

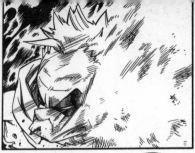

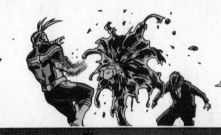

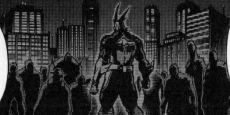

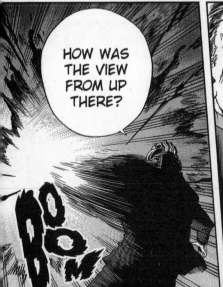

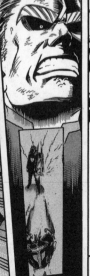

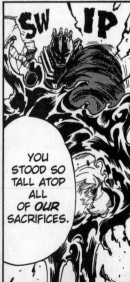

DETROIT
SMASH!!!!!!!!!
GHAK
HE NEGATED MY ATTACK WITH SHEER FORCE...
YOU STILL CAN'T ...
...FIGHT AT FULL POWER, HUH?
BECAUSE FOR HEROES, THERE ARE OH SO MANY THINGS...

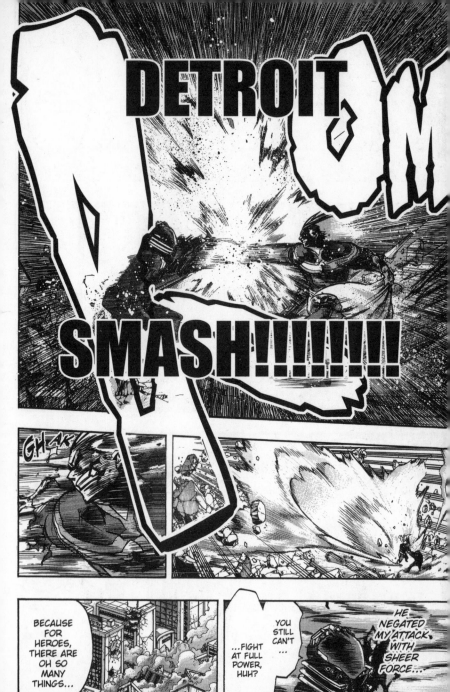

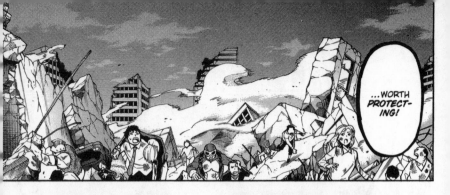

...WORTH PROTECT-ING!
SHUT UP!
!
THAT'S WHAT YOU DO. YOU TOY WITH PEOPLE'S VERY LIVES!
KRAK KRAK
YOU BREAK THEM!
YOU STEAL FROM THEM!
YOU TAKE ADVANTAGE AND MANIPU-LATE THEM!
DAMN... CAN'T WARP ANYMORE...
FWIP
YOU SNEER AT THEM, WHEN THEY'RE JUST TRYING TO LIVE THEIR EVERYDAY LIVES!
AND FOR THAT...

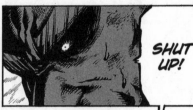

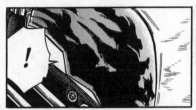

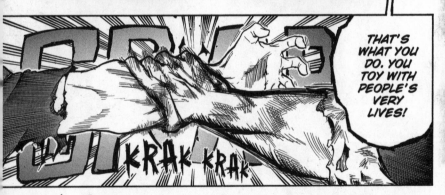

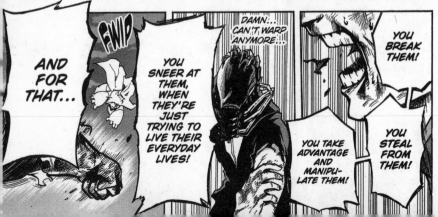

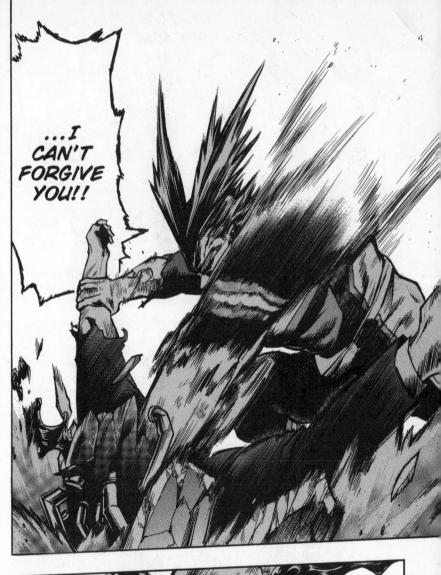

...I
CAN'T
FORGIVE
YOU!!

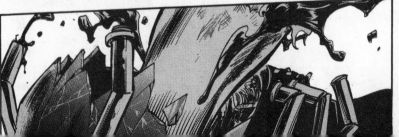

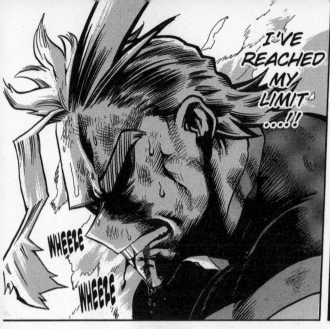

TOSHINORI ...!
I'VE REACHED MY LIMIT ...!!
WHEEZE
WHEEZE
GETTING AWFULLY EMOTIONAL, AREN'T YOU, ALL MIGHT?
I SEEM TO REMEMBER HEARING THAT EXACT LINE ONCE BEFORE.
CHF
CHF
FROM THE PREVIOUS PERSON TO INHERIT ONE FOR ALL...
SQUISH
NANA SHIMURA.

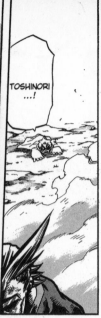

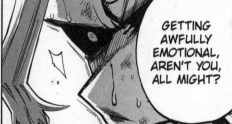

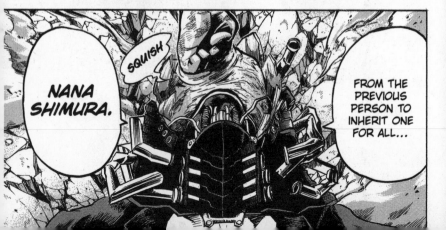

MY HERO ACADEMIA

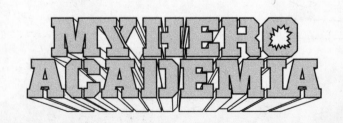

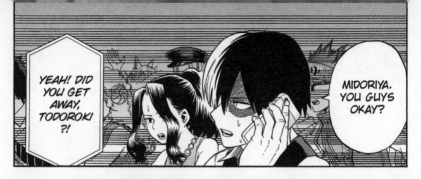

MIDORIYA. YOU GUYS OKAY?
YEAH! DID YOU GET AWAY, TODOROKI?!
No. 92 - ONE FOR ALL
I THINK SO... WE RAN BEHIND ALL FOR ONE AND BUMPED INTO SOME PROS HELPING EVERYONE EVACUATE.
NICE!
WE'RE OVER BY THE STATION, MORE THAN LIKELY OUT OF RANGE OF THAT SHOCK WAVE ATTACK!
THE RESCUE WAS SUCCESS-FUL!
WH OOOP
WAHHHH!
LISTEN UP! IT'S NOT LIKE I GOT SAVED OR ANYTHING!
YOU GUYS JUST HAPPENED TO BE THE BEST OPTION I HAD!
GOOD CHOICE!
MOSTLY, I JUST DIDN'T WANNA...
...GET IN ALL MIGHT'S WAY.

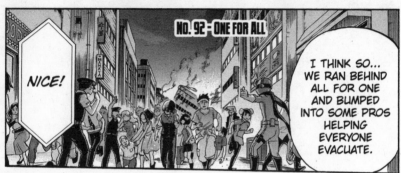

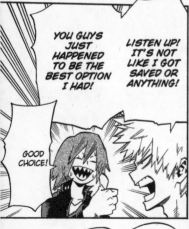

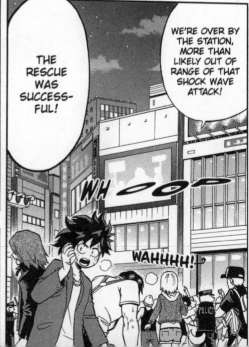

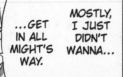

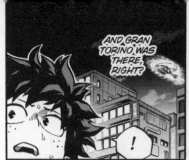

RIGHT... GIVING HIM ROOM TO FIGHT.
THAT WAS THE BEST STRATEGY WE HAD...
AND GRAN TORINO WAS THERE, RIGHT?
!
HELICOPTERS... PROBABLY THE PRESS...!
DID WE DO THE RIGHT THING...?
HE'S ...
...GONNA BE OKAY, RIGHT?! ALL MIGHT ...!
FROM THE PREVIOUS PERSON TO INHERIT ONE FOR ALL...
NANA SHIMURA.

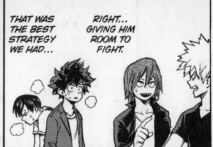

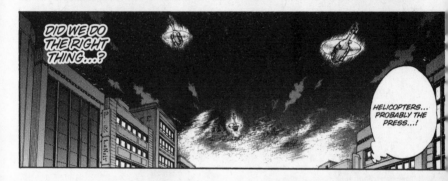

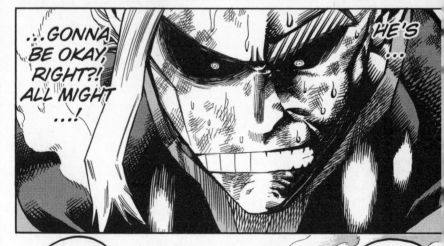

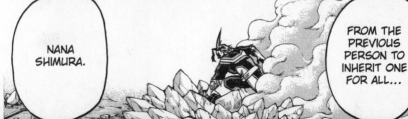

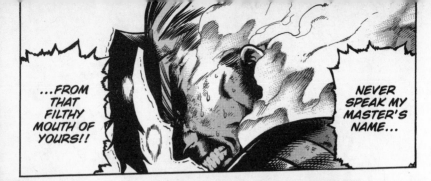

NEVER SPEAK MY MASTER'S NAME...
...FROM THAT FILTHY MOUTH OF YOURS!!
TAKE PRIDE, TOSHI-NORI!
YOU'RE NOT LIKE THE OTHERS, WHO'RE BORN WITH WHAT THEY HAVE.
YOU WORKED HARD TO WIN YOUR POWER!
THAT FOOL OF A WOMAN PUT HER STUPID IDEALS FIRST, WITHOUT THE POWER TO BACK THEM UP! IT WAS PRETTY EMBARRASSING FOR ME, AS THE FATHER OF ONE FOR ALL. AND THEN SHE DIED SUCH A PATHETIC DEATH. WHERE DO I BEGIN, REALLY...?
Enough!!

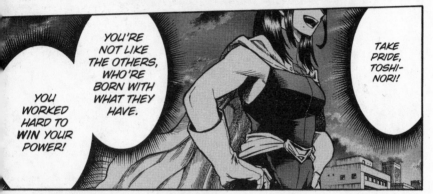

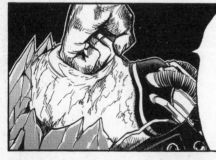

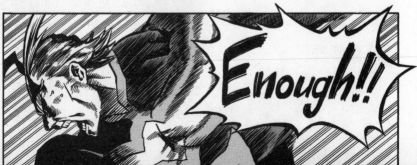

FWOOM!

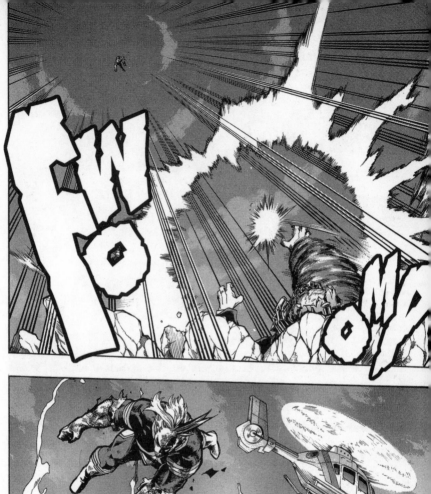

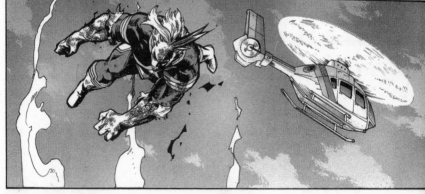

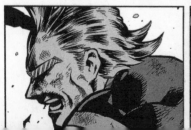

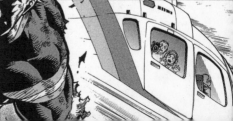

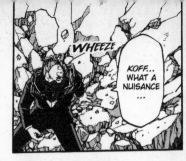

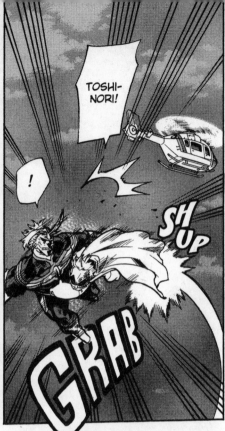

TOSHI-NORI!
!
SHUP
GRAB
WHEEZE
KOFF... WHAT A NUISANCE ...
THIS IS JUST LIKE SIX YEARS AGO!
CALM DOWN!! DON'T DANCE TO HIS TUNE!
HE MANAGED TO GET AWAY LAST TIME... RIGHT AFTER OPENING THAT HOLE IN YOUR GUT!
KRASH
HE KNOWS *THIS* IS YOUR WEAKNESS, SO DON'T GIVE HIM A CHANCE TO TALK!
RIGHT ...

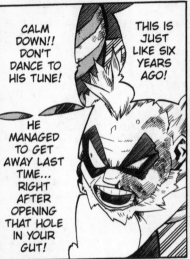

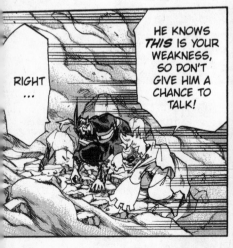

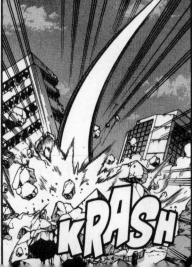

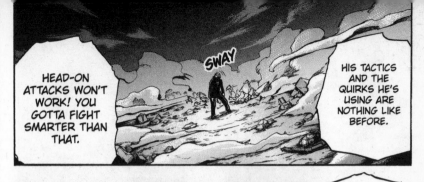

HIS TACTICS AND THE QUIRKS HE'S USING ARE NOTHING LIKE BEFORE.
SWAY
HEAD-ON ATTACKS WON'T WORK! YOU GOTTA FIGHT SMARTER THAN THAT.
YOU CAN STILL MOVE, YEAH?! SMASH PAST YOUR LIMIT! THIS IS DO-OR-DIE!!
WHEEZE
WHEEZE
RIGHT!
WE'RE HERE AT THIS NIGHTMARISH SCENE! HALF OF KAMINO WARD WAS DESTROYED IN THE BLINK OF AN EYE!
ALL MIGHT IS CURRENTLY EXCHANGING BLOWS WITH THE PURPORTED VILLAIN BEHIND ALL THIS DESTRUCTION!
IT'S HARD TO BELIEVE THAT A SINGLE VILLAIN COULD OBLITERATE SEVERAL CITY BLOCKS AND GO TOE-TO-TOE WITH THE SYMBOL OF PEACE HIMSELF...
HE GOT THE DROP ON THEM!
TSUKA-UCHI... ALL MIGHT!
WHOA! THAT LOOKS BAD.

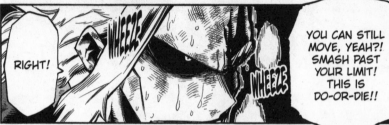

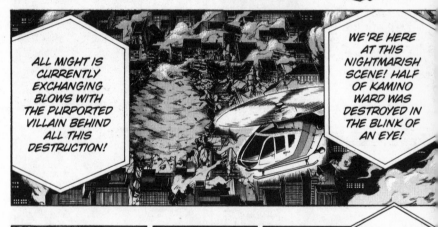

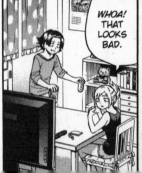

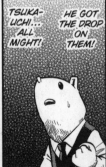

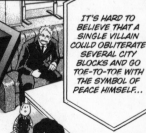

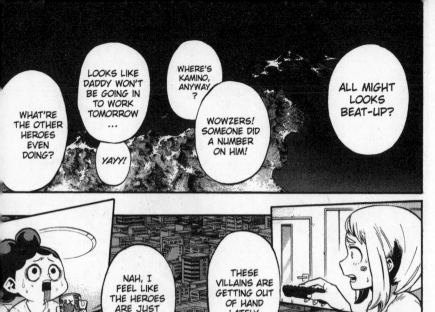

ALL MIGHT LOOKS BEAT-UP?
WOWZERS! SOMEONE DID A NUMBER ON HIM!
WHERE'S KAMINO, ANYWAY?
LOOKS LIKE DADDY WON'T BE GOING IN TO WORK TOMORROW...
YAYY!
WHAT'RE THE OTHER HEROES EVEN DOING?
THESE VILLAINS ARE GETTING OUT OF HAND LATELY.
NAH, I FEEL LIKE THE HEROES ARE JUST SLACKING.
THEY'RE GETTING SLOPPY!!
THAT'S JUST HOW IT IS SOMETIMES.
YEAH, BUT STILL...
I'M SURE ALL MIGHT CAN PULL IT OFF, IN THE END!
TOMURA'S BEEN WORKING SO DILIGENTLY TO ERODE THE TRUST IN YOU HEROES.
I ALMOST FEEL BAD PUTTING THE NAIL IN THE COFFIN...

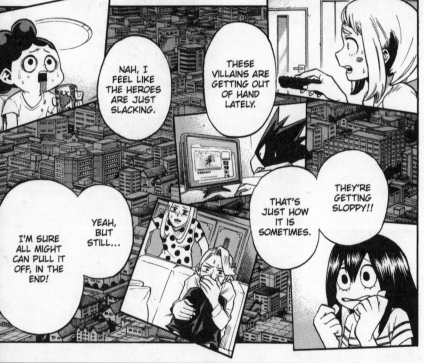

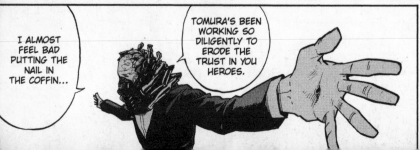

HEY, ALL MIGHT.
JUST AS YOU HATE ME...
I, TOO, DESPISE YOU.
IT'S TRUE, I MAY HAVE KILLED YOUR MASTER, BUT...
YOU SMASHED EVERYTHING I WORKED SO HARD TO BUILD.
THAT'S WHY I'M HOPING TO SEE YOU DIE AN UGLY, BRUTAL DEATH!!
GWOOOM
THERE'S A BIG ONE COMING!
DODGE AND COUNTER-ATTACK!
BOOD
DODGE? CAN YOU AFFORD TO?
CHF

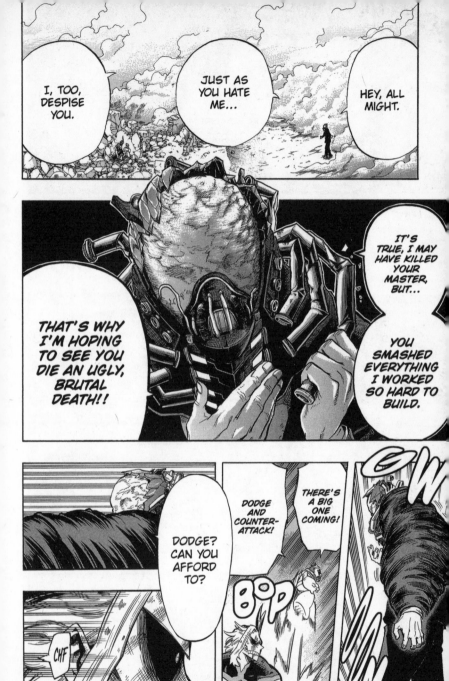

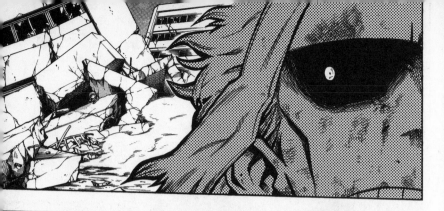

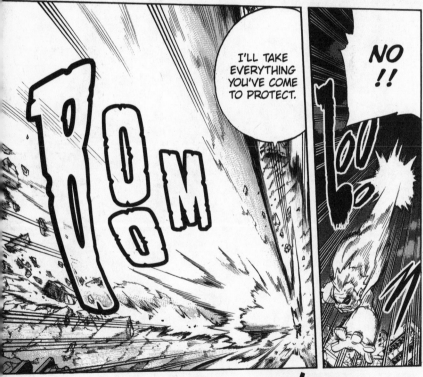

NO !!
I'LL TAKE EVERYTHING YOU'VE COME TO PROTECT.
BOOM
WHOO
GUH ...!!
FIRST YOUR *IMAGE*, WHICH YOU'VE MAINTAINED DESPITE YOUR WOUND.
THEN YOUR *PRIDE*...
WHOOSH

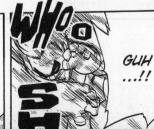

THE WORLD WILL SEE YOU FOR THE PATHETIC MAN YOU ARE.
THEIR *SYMBOL* OF PEACE.
LIVE

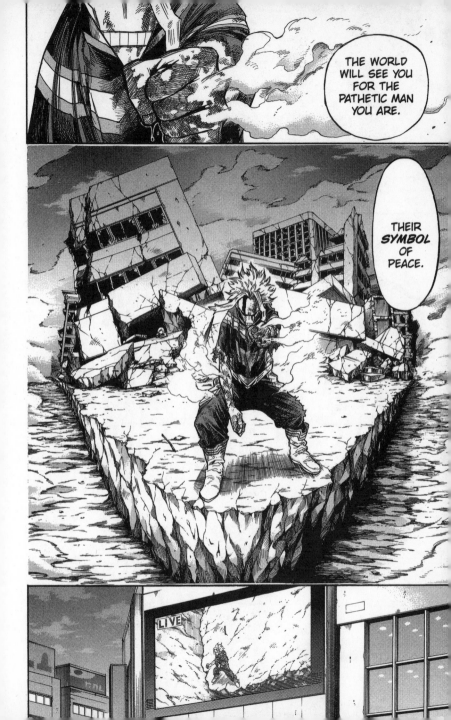

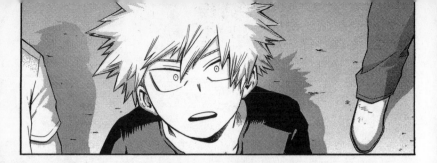

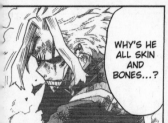

HUH?
OH...
WHY'S HE ALL SKIN AND BONES...?
UM... WHAT'S... HUH...? A-ARE YOU SEEING THIS, VIEWERS?
ALL MIGHT... HE'S ALL SHRIVELED UP...
PLEASE DON'T BROADCAST THIS TO THE WORLD.
PLEASE DON'T LET THE WORLD SEE THIS, PLEASE.
NO...
THE SYMBOL OF PEACE, WHO SAVES PEOPLE WITH A SMILE...
...CAN'T BE SEEN SUC-CUMBING TO EVIL.
HIS... SECRET...
THOSE HOLLOW CHEEKS AND SUNKEN EYES... THE TOP HERO'S LOOKING A LITTLE WORSE FOR WEAR, I'D SAY.
AW, DON'T BE ASHAMED. THAT'S YOUR TRUE FORM, ISN'T IT?!

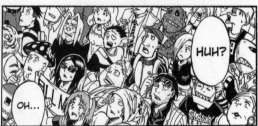

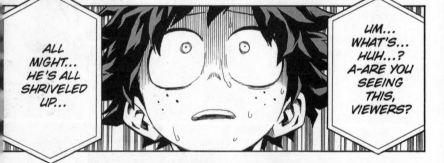

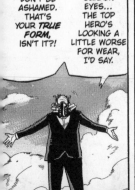

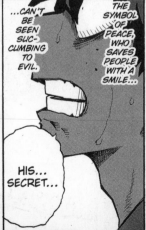

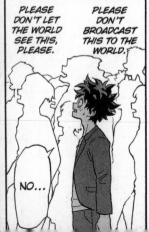

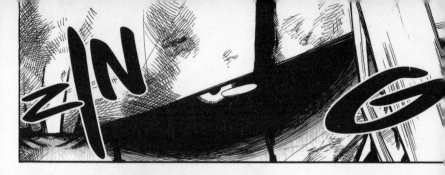

ZING
I SEE...
MY BODY MAY WITHER AWAY... YOU MIGHT EXPOSE ME TO THE WORLD...
BUT MY SPIRIT ...
...IS WHAT MAKES ME THE SYMBOL OF PEACE !!
YOU HAVEN'T STOLEN AWAY ONE BIT OF THAT!!
WONDER-FUL!
WHEEZE
WHEEZE
YOU'RE JUST LIKE A STUBBORN CHILD. BUT I'VE FORGOTTEN SOMETHING.
I WONDER IF *THIS* IS ENOUGH TO BREAK THAT SPIRIT OF YOURS... PERHAPS...

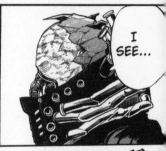

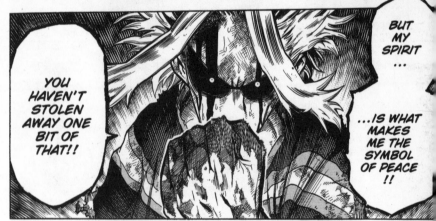

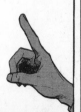

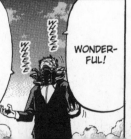

TOMURA SHIGARAKI IS NANA SHIMURA'S GRANDSON.

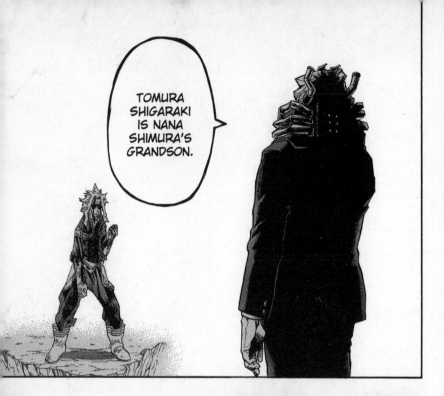

AND HE'S *HATED* YOU THIS WHOLE TIME.

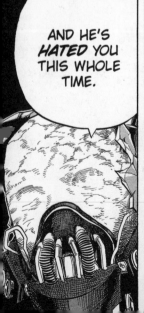

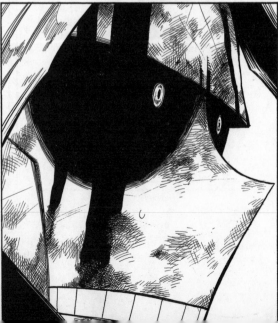

I'VE ENGINEERED THESE ENCOUNTERS BETWEEN YOU TWO.
AND YOU DEFEATED HIM SOUNDLY.
YOU WON, WITH A SMILE.
SO PROUD, DESPITE YOUR IGNORANCE.
YOU'RE LYING...
NOPE. YOU KNOW IT TO BE TRUE...
...BECAUSE IT'S JUST THE KIND OF THING I'D DO.
HUH...? WHAT'S THE MATTER, ALL MIGHT?
TUG
TUG
WHERE'S THAT WINNING SMILE OF YOURS?
WHEN YOU HAVE TO SAVE SOMEONE, THEY'RE USUALLY IN A SCARY SITUATION.
A TRUE HERO SAVES NOT ONLY THEIR LIVES, BUT ALSO THEIR SPIRITS... THAT'S WHAT I BELIEVE.

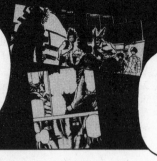

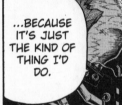

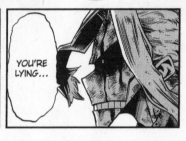

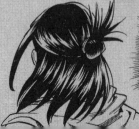

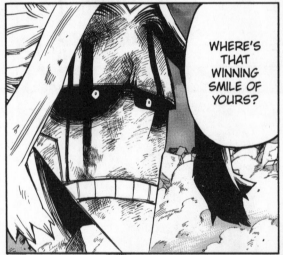

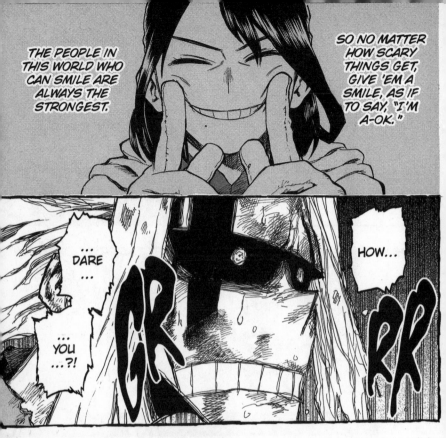

SO NO MATTER HOW SCARY THINGS GET, GIVE 'EM A SMILE, AS IF TO SAY, "I'M A-OK."
THE PEOPLE IN THIS WORLD WHO CAN SMILE ARE ALWAYS THE STRONGEST.
HOW...
... DARE ... ... YOU ...?!
GR RR
OOH... WHAT FUN!
LOOKS LIKE I MANAGED TO STEAL THAT ONE BIT, ANYWAY.
MY MASTER'S OWN FAMILY...
HE...!!
WHAT...
...HAVE I DONE?
AHHHHH!!

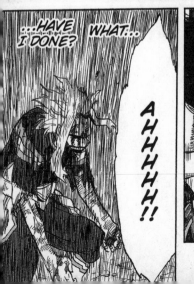

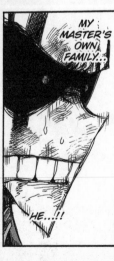

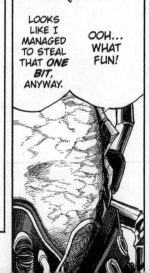

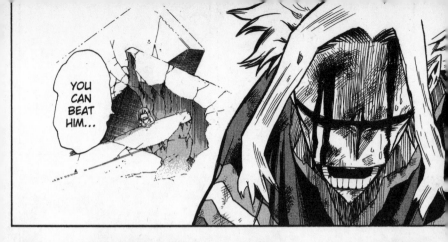

YOU CAN BEAT HIM...

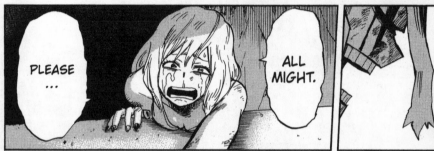

PLEASE ...

ALL MIGHT.

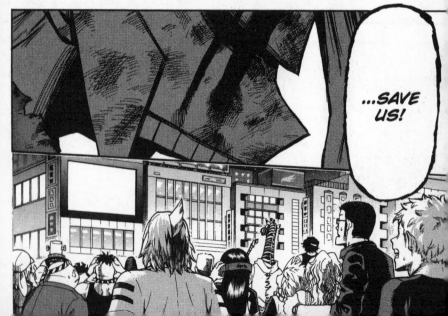

...SAVE US!

ALL MIGHT...
THIS LOOKS BAD...!!
WIN...
WHISPER
BUT... NO...
ALL MIGHT...!
IF YOU DON'T BEAT THIS GUY...
...I DON'T THINK ANYONE CAN...
HE MIGHT LOOK DIFFERENT, BUT HE'S STILL OUR ALL MIGHT, RIGHT?!
HE ALWAYS MANAGES TO COME OUT ON TOP!
YOU CAN DO IT, ALL MIGHT!
D-DON'T YOU DARE LOSE, ALL MIGHT!!
RAAWR
YOU CAN DO IT!!!
FLIP

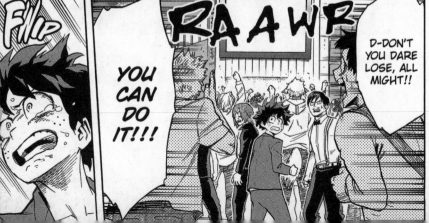

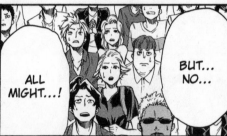

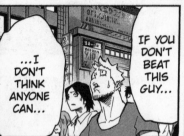

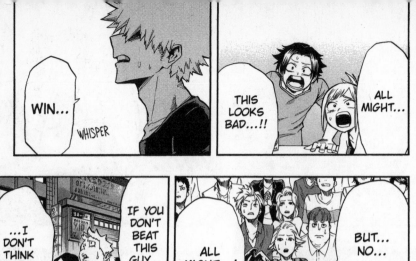

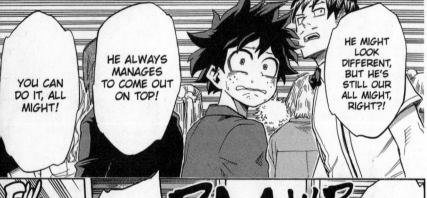

YOU CAN WIN... ALL MIGHT!!

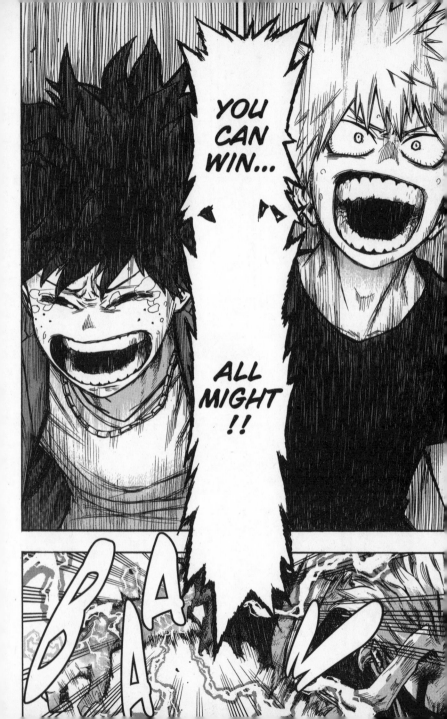

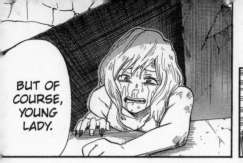

BUT OF COURSE, YOUNG LADY.
INDEED!
THERE ARE PLENTY OF THINGS...
...THAT HEROES NEED TO PROTECT, ALL FOR ONE!!
FWOOO
THAT'S WHY...
...I CAN'T LOSE.

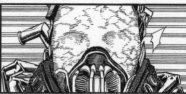

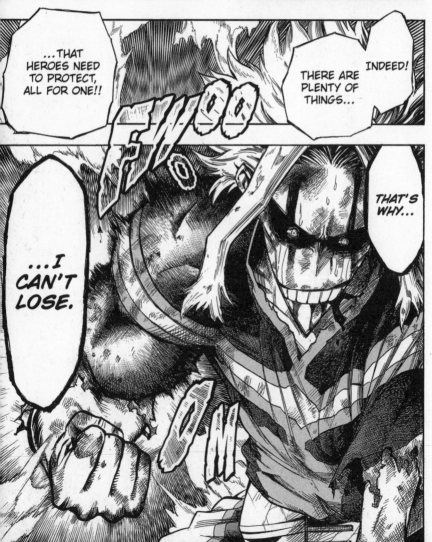

MY HERO ACADEMIA

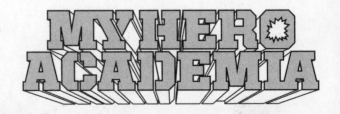

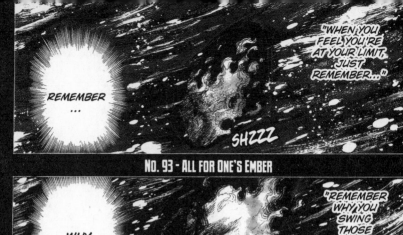

"WHEN YOU FEEL YOU'RE AT YOUR LIMIT, JUST REMEMBER..."
REMEMBER ...
SHZZZ
No. 93 - ALL FOR ONE'S EMBER
"REMEMBER WHY YOU SWING THOSE FISTS."
WHY I...
SHZZZ
"I'M TALKING ABOUT WHERE YOU STARTED! THAT'S WHAT YOU NEED TO RECALL..."
"...IN ORDER TO PUSH YOURSELF THAT MUCH FURTHER PAST YOUR LIMIT!"
I WANT TO MAKE THE WORLD A PLACE WHERE EVERYONE CAN LIVE WITH A SMILE.
AND FOR THAT... THE WORLD NEEDS A SYMBOL.

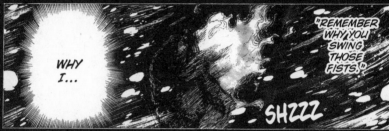

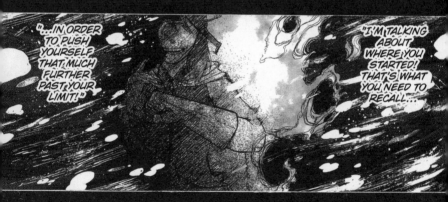

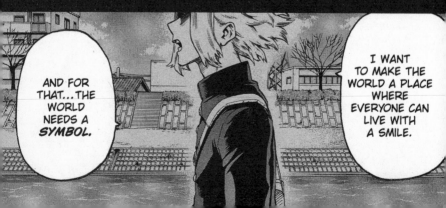

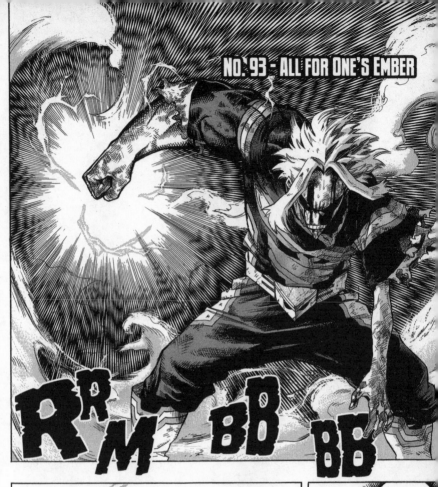

No. 93 - All For One's Ember
RRM BBD BB
YOU CAN STILL MOVE, YEAH?! SMASH PAST YOUR LIMIT!
YOWCH...
CHF...
HE'S HAD TO COUNTER A LOT OF MASSIVE ATTACKS LIKE THAT ONE... HE'S ALREADY GONE WAY PAST HIS LIMIT...
HIS BODY'S UNSTABLE. HE CAN ONLY KEEP HIS RIGHT ARM IN MUSCLE FORM AT THIS POINT...

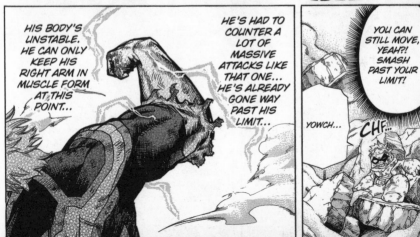

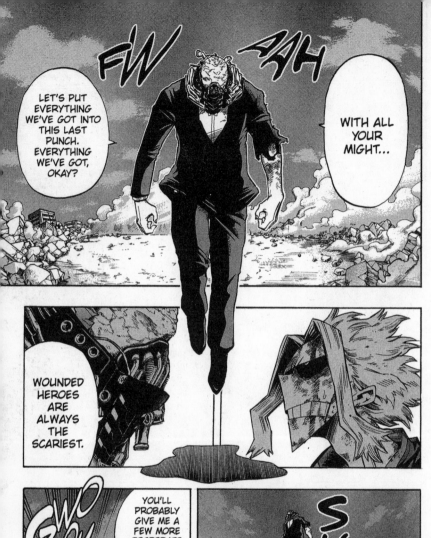

FWAAH
WITH ALL YOUR MIGHT...
LET'S PUT EVERYTHING WE'VE GOT INTO THIS LAST PUNCH. EVERYTHING WE'VE GOT, OKAY?
WOUNDED HEROES ARE ALWAYS THE SCARIEST.
SHAA
AFTER I RIPPED YOUR GUTS OUT... THE LOOK ON YOUR FACE WHEN YOU CHARGED AT ME...
I STILL SEE IT IN MY NIGHT-MARES SOME-TIMES.
YOU'LL PROBABLY GIVE ME A FEW MORE DESPERATE PUNCHES, SO I SHOULD PREPARE MYSELF.
GWOOM

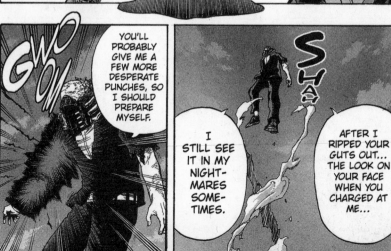

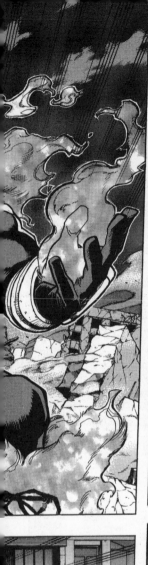

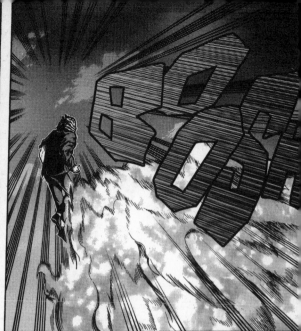

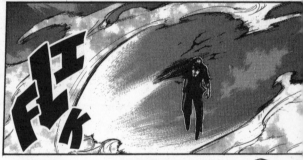

FLI
K

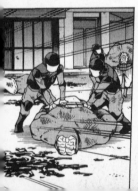

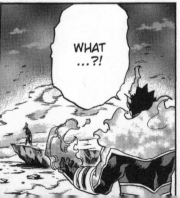

WHAT
...?!

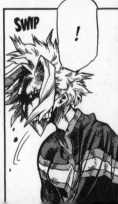

SWIP

!

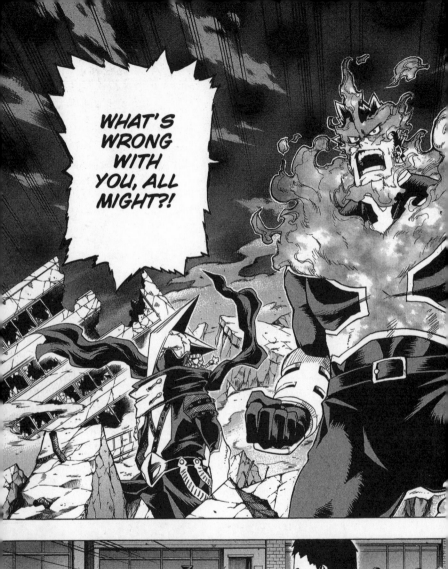

WHAT'S WRONG WITH YOU, ALL MIGHT?!

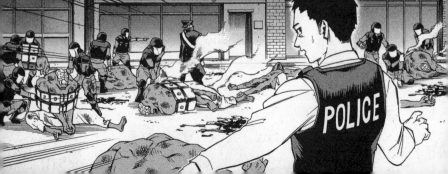

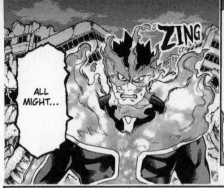

THEY MIGHT'VE ONLY BEEN MIDLEVEL ONES, BUT STILL...
CLEANING UP ALL THOSE NOMU SO QUICKLY... GUESS I SHOULD'VE EXPECTED NO LESS FROM NO. 2.
YOU SURE HAVE CLIMBED HIGH.
ZING
ALL MIGHT...
ALL THIS EFFORT, JUST TO BEAT YOU...!
BUT THE MORE I TRAINED, THE MORE OBVIOUS IT WAS.
THE GAP BETWEEN US...
HOW I WAS ALWAYS LAGGING BEHIND...!
THAT DESPAIR!!
IT LED ME TO...
EXPLAIN THIS...
...PATHETIC STATE YOU'RE IN!

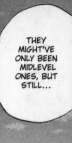

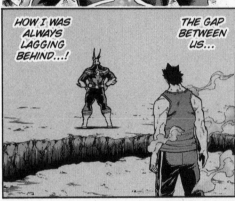

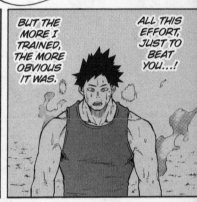

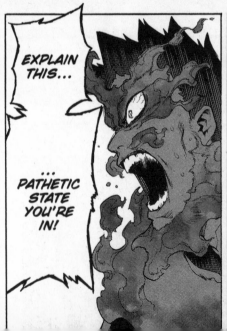

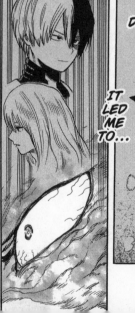

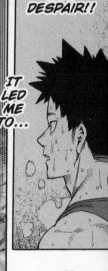

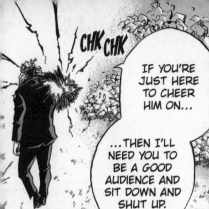

CHK CHK
IF YOU'RE JUST HERE TO CHEER HIM ON...
...THEN I'LL NEED YOU TO BE A GOOD AUDIENCE AND SIT DOWN AND SHUT UP.
SH SHK
NOT SO FAST, YOU DESTROYER.
SWIP
WE'RE HERE TO DO SOME *SAVING!*

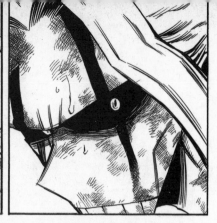

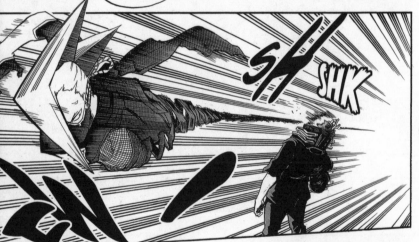

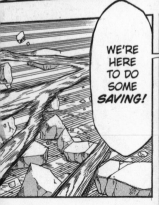

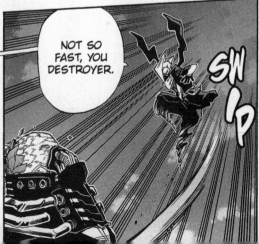

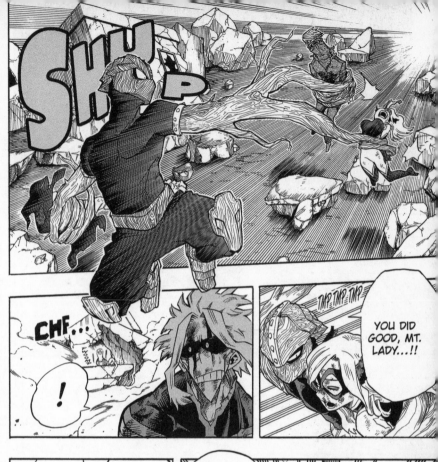

SHUP
TMP TMP TMP
YOU DID GOOD, MT. LADY...!!
CHF...
!
EVEN IF... THIS IS ALL WE CAN DO...
WORMP
Grab on to me!
HFF
WE'LL DO WHATEVER WE CAN TO EASE YOUR BURDEN...
TIGER ...!

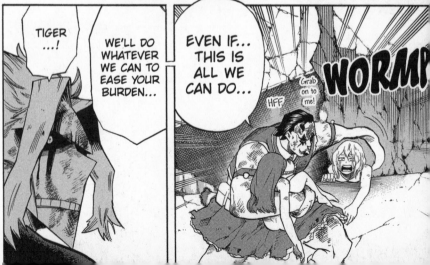

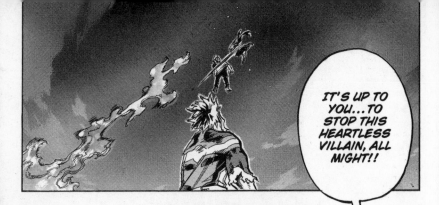

IT'S UP TO YOU...TO STOP THIS HEARTLESS VILLAIN, ALL MIGHT!!
WE'RE ALL ROOTING FOR YOU!!
NO MATTER HOW YOU LOOK, YOU'RE STILL OUR NO. 1 HERO!
TOSHI-NORI YAGI?
HE'S AN INTERESTING ONE. A LITTLE CRAZY.
ACCORDING TO HIM...CRIME'S NOT DECLINING BECAUSE THE PEOPLE DON'T HAVE ANYONE TO RELY ON.
IT'S BECAUSE THIS COUNTRY'S GOT NO "PILLAR" TO SUPPORT IT...
...SO HE SAYS HE'S GONNA BE THAT PILLAR.

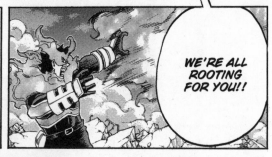

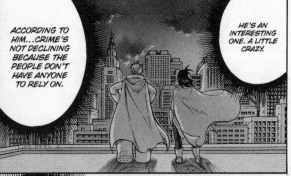

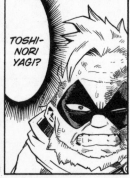

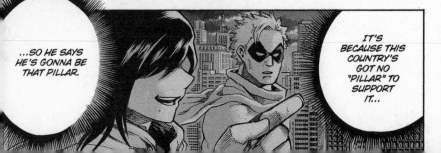

EVERYONE'S RESTING ALL THEIR HOPES...
...ON YOUR VICTORY!

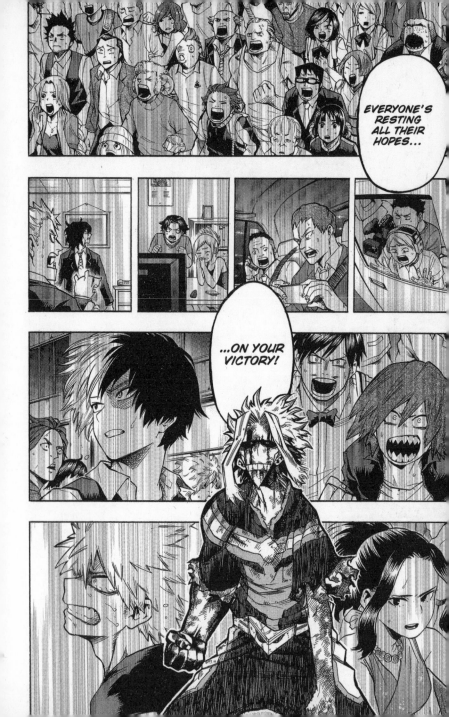

DOOOOM
OH, PLEASE ...
"SPIRIT" THIS, "HOPE" THAT...
WAKE UP. THIS IS REALITY.
FWIP
GWOOM

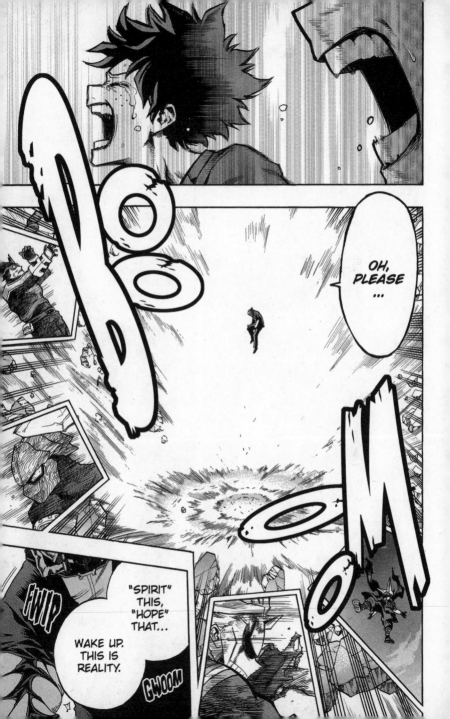

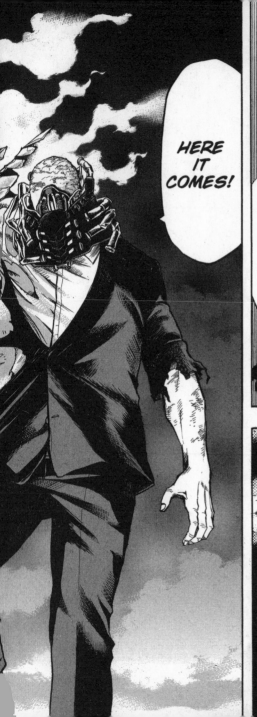

HERE IT COMES!

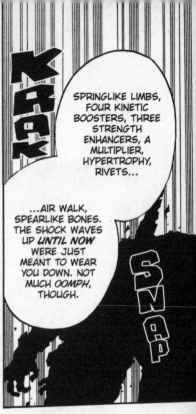

KRAK

SPRINGLIKE LIMBS, FOUR KINETIC BOOSTERS, THREE STRENGTH ENHANCERS, A MULTIPLIER, HYPERTROPHY, RIVETS...

...AIR WALK, SPEARLIKE BONES. THE SHOCK WAVES UP *UNTIL NOW* WERE JUST MEANT TO WEAR YOU DOWN. NOT MUCH *OOMPH*, THOUGH.

SNAP

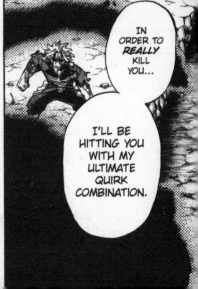

IN ORDER TO *REALLY* KILL YOU...

I'LL BE HITTING YOU WITH MY ULTIMATE QUIRK COMBINATION.

TRADING BLOWS WITH YOU EARLIER WAS ENOUGH TO FINALLY CONFIRM MY SUSPICIONS, ALL MIGHT.
ZOOM
YOU NO LONGER POSSESS ONE FOR ALL.
WHAT YOU'RE USING NOW IS AN AFTER-THOUGHT... MERE DREGS... THE EMBER THAT REMAINED AFTER THE TRANSFER.
AND THAT EMBER GETS DIMMER EVERY TIME YOU DRAW ON IT...
A WEAK GUTTERING LIGHT THAT DOESN'T EVEN NEED BLOWING OUT. IT'LL SOON DIE ON ITS OWN...

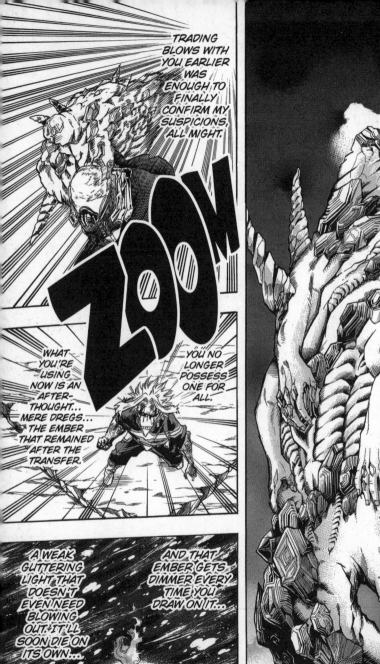

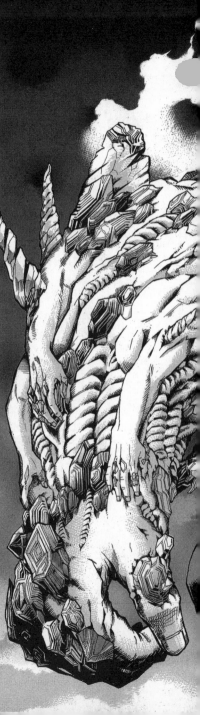

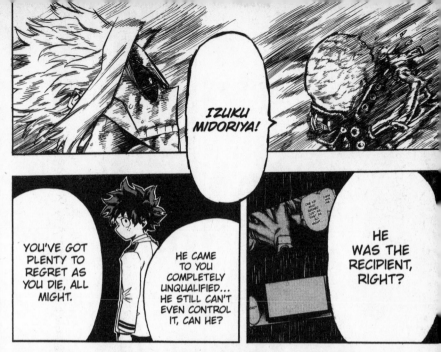

IZUKU MIDORIYA!
THERE WAS ONE.
ONE KID WHO SEEMED JUST AS FAST AS ALL MIGHT...
HE WAS THE RECIPIENT, RIGHT?
HE CAME TO YOU COMPLETELY UNQUALIFIED... HE STILL CAN'T EVEN CONTROL IT, CAN HE?
YOU'VE GOT PLENTY TO REGRET AS YOU DIE, ALL MIGHT.
BECAUSE YOU'VE ALSO FAILED...
...AS A TEACHER!

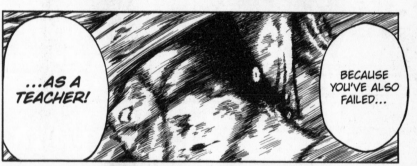

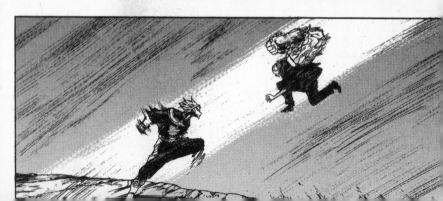

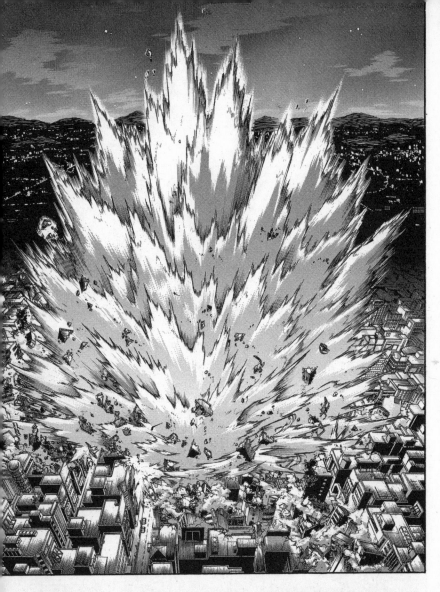

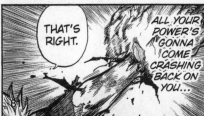

THAT'S RIGHT.

ALL YOUR POWER'S GONNA COME CRASHING BACK ON YOU...

...RECOIL!

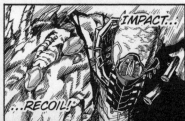

IMPACT...

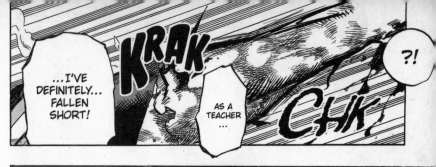

?!
KRAK
CHK
AS A TEACHER...
...I'VE DEFINITELY... FALLEN SHORT!
AND I'M WILLING...
...TO ACCEPT THAT!!
KRK
KRK
KRK
I SEE...
PA-THETIC.
YOUR DYING EMBER...
...WILL GO OUT, ALL ON ITS OWN.

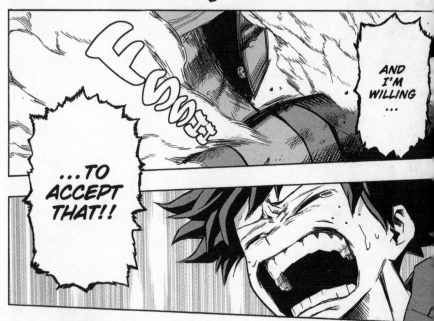

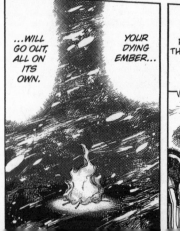

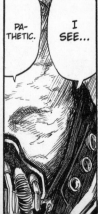

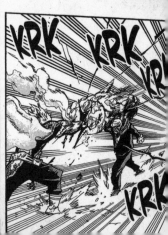

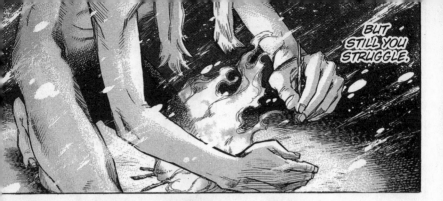

BUT STILL YOU STRUGGLE.
UNTIL YOUR JOB ON THIS EARTH IS DONE, YOU'LL KEEP IT ALIVE...
STRUGGLING DESPERATELY TO KEEP IT GOING.
WHEN YOU FEEL YOU'RE AT YOUR LIMIT, JUST REMEMBER...
I'M MORE THAN JUST THE SYMBOL!!
JUST AS MY MASTER WAS THERE FOR ME...

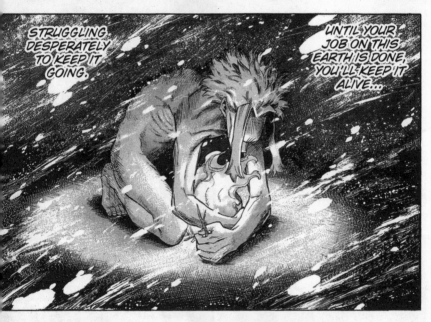

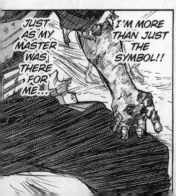

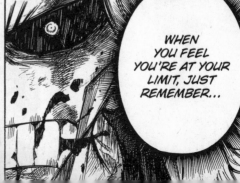

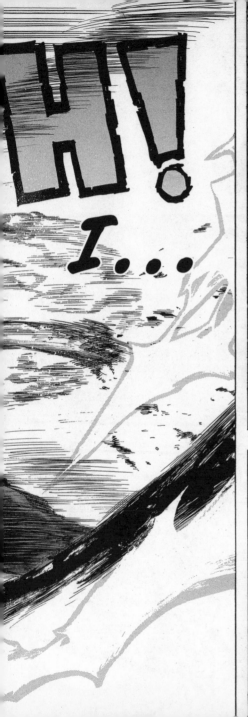

**H!**

I....

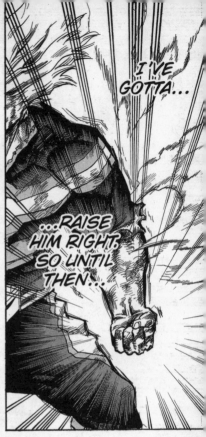

I'VE GOTTA...

...RAISE HIM RIGHT, SO UNTIL THEN...

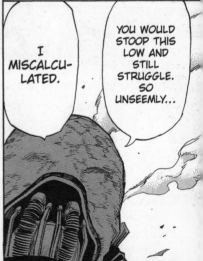

YOU WOULD STOOP THIS LOW AND STILL STRUGGLE. SO UNSEEMLY...

I MISCALCU-LATED.

SMAS
...CAN'T DIE !!!!

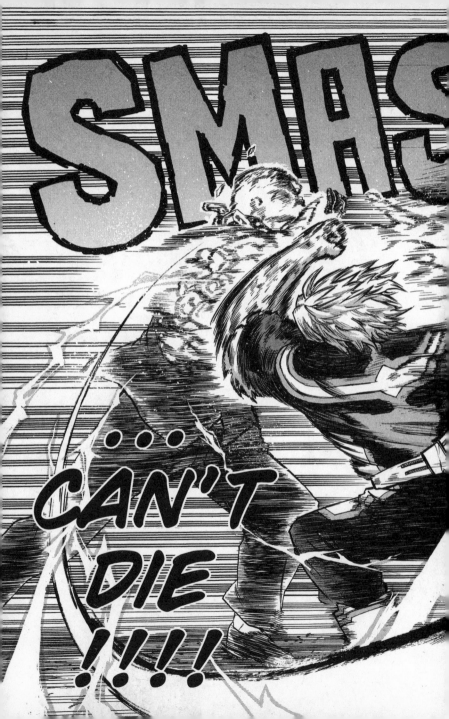

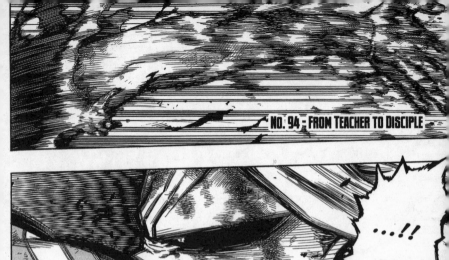

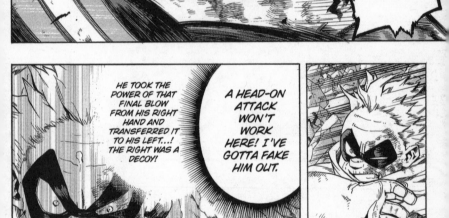

No. 94 - From Teacher to Disciple
...!!
A HEAD-ON ATTACK WON'T WORK HERE! I'VE GOTTA FAKE HIM OUT.
HE TOOK THE POWER OF THAT FINAL BLOW FROM HIS RIGHT HAND AND TRANSFERRED IT TO HIS LEFT...! THE RIGHT WAS A DECOY!
BUT...!

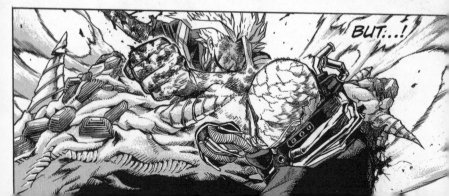

PETTY TRICKS? HOW UNLIKE YOU.
WHOSE INFLUENCE IS THAT, I WONDER?
BULGE
BOOF
TOO WEAK.

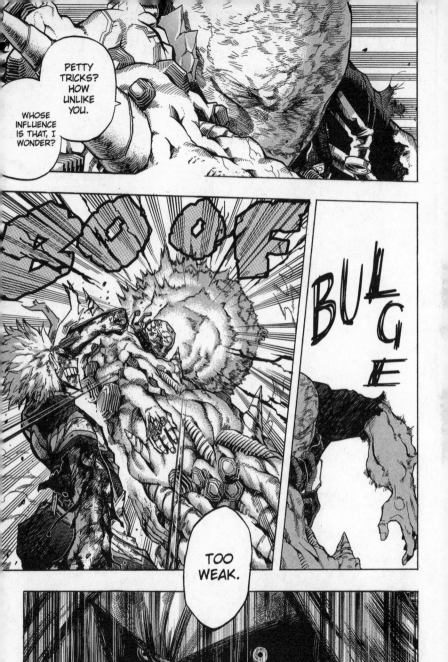

THAT'S BECAUSE ...
!
BULGE
...I DIDN'T...
...PUT MY BACK INTO IT!!

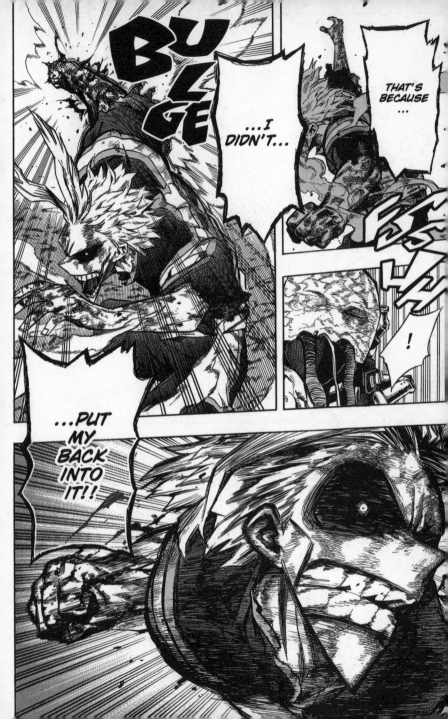

SO MANY HAVE ALREADY PASSED THIS POWER DOWN FROM ONE TO ANOTHER.
IN ORDER TO SERVE THE GREATER GOOD... IN ORDER TO CREATE HOPE FOR EVERYONE.
AND NOW IT'S YOUR TURN.
"DO YOUR BEST, TOSHINORI."
GRIT

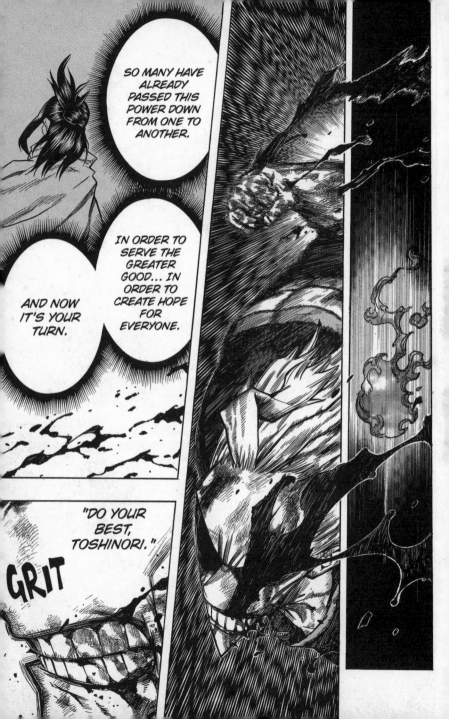

SAY GOOD-BYE...
AHHHHHHHHH

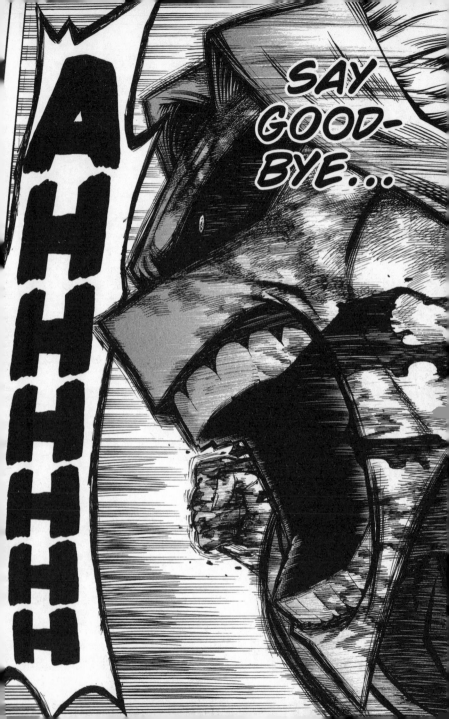

...ALL FOR ONE.

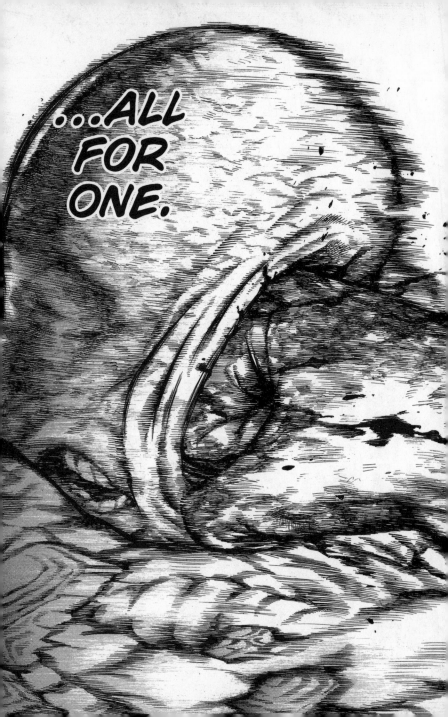

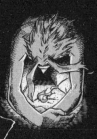

STATES OF

FARE-
WELL
...

ASH

UNITED
SM
ONE FOR ALL!

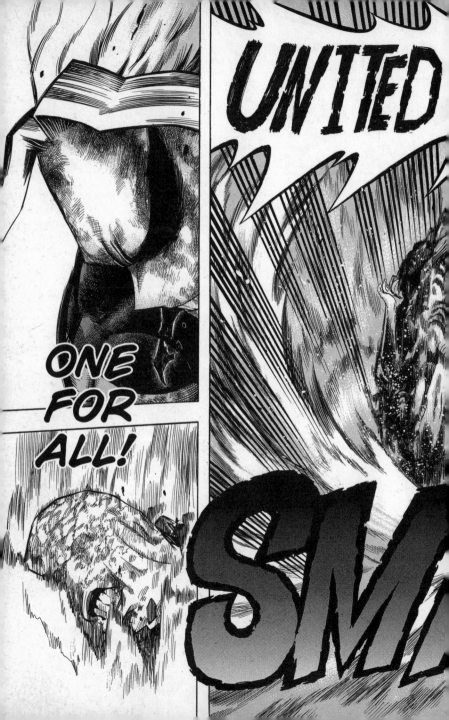

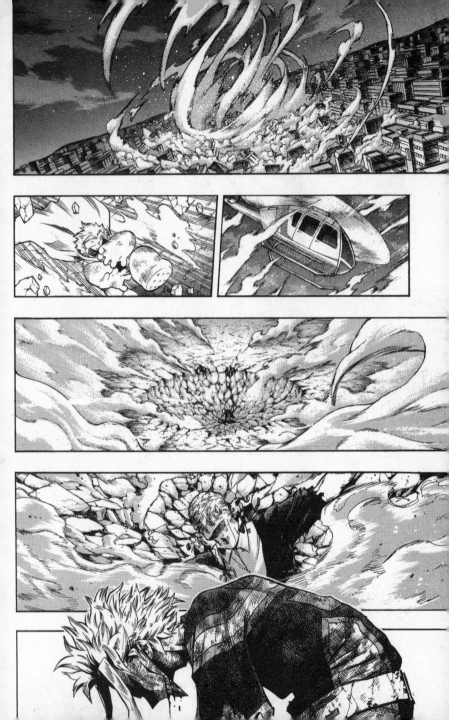

WORMP
SHF
AH...
!!

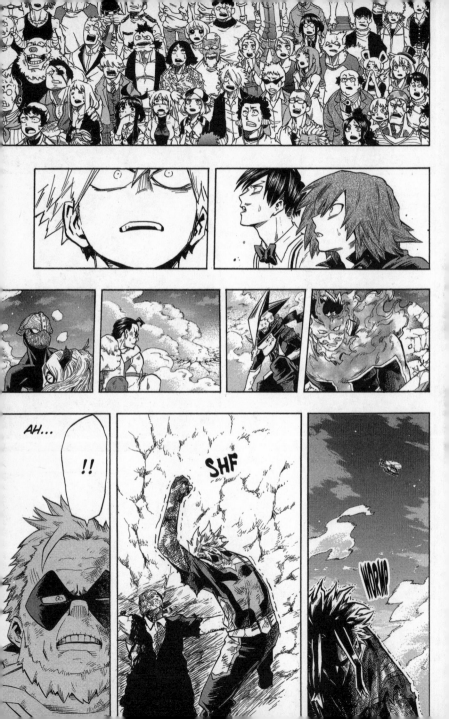

ALL MIGHT !!
FWO OM
THE VILLAIN...IS OUT COLD!! HE WON!! ALL MIGHT WON!!
WORMP
HE REALLY WON!! HE'S STILL STANDING!!!
WHOA...! HE'S GONNA OVERDO IT...
WAIT... JUST LET HIM.
THIS COUNTRY'S GOT NO "PILLAR" TO SUPPORT IT...

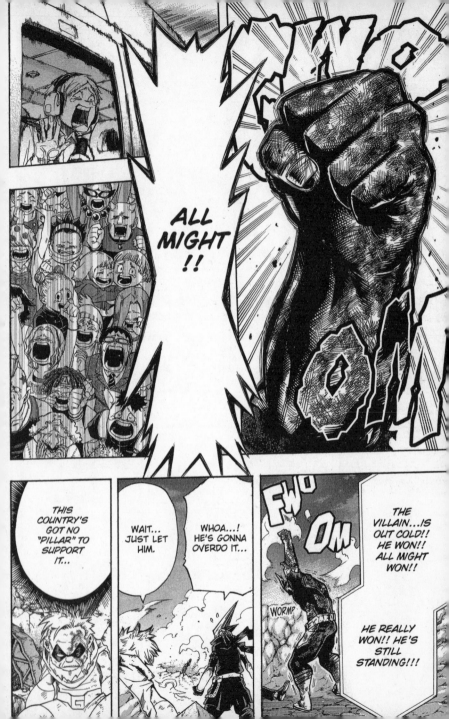

...SO HE SAYS HE'S GONNA BE THAT PILLAR.
HE'S STILL ON THE JOB.
THE SYMBOL OF PEACE...
HIS FINAL ACT...
...AS THE NUMBER ONE HERO...

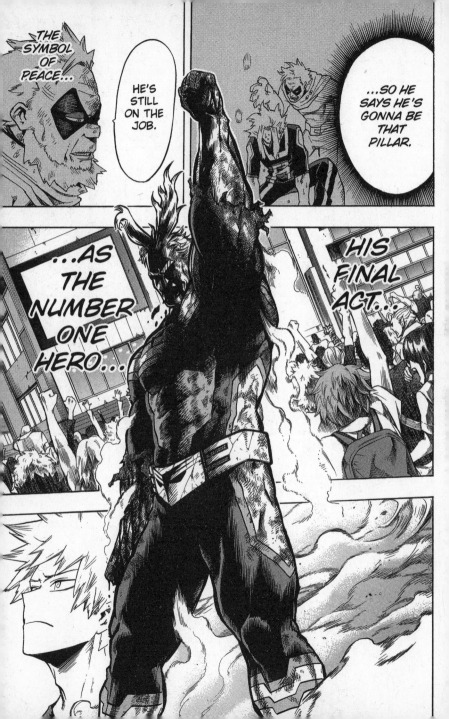

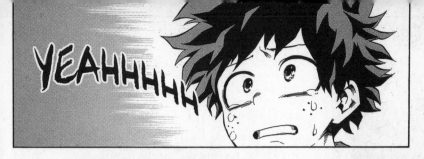

YEAHHHHH
UNDER HERE! TWO MORE PEOPLE!! OVER THERE TOO!
GOT IT! LET'S HURRY!
THE HEROES' RESCUE EFFORTS THAT BEGAN DURING ALL MIGHT'S BATTLE CONTINUE IN THE AFTERMATH.
WE EXPECT A SIGNIFICANT NUMBER OF CASUALTIES...!!
THE VILLAIN BEHIND THIS CATASTROPHE IS...AH, AT THIS *VERY MOMENT*...!!
*THE VILLAIN IS BEING LOADED INTO AN IRON MAIDEN! WE CAN SEE THAT ALL MIGHT AND COMPANY ARE TAKING ALL PRECAUTIONS!*
KOFF

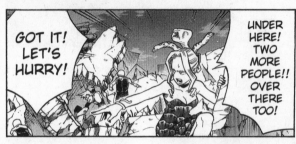

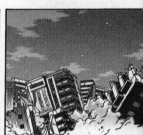

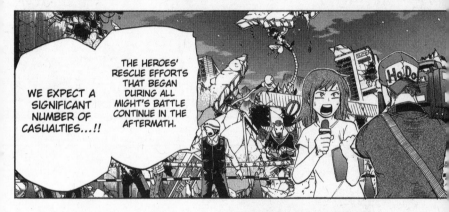

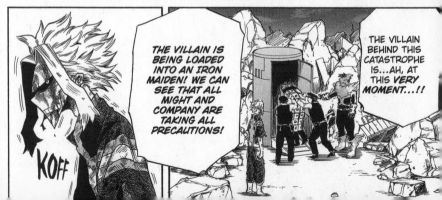

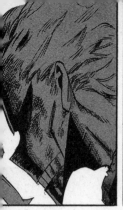

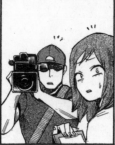

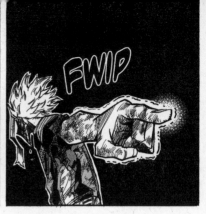

FWIP
WE'RE HANDING OUT BLANKETS OVER HERE!
THE TRAINS ARE OUT, SO THOSE SEEKING FIRST AID FACILITIES SHOULD COME THIS WAY. DON'T STOP MOVING. SLOWLY AND ORDERLY, NOW...
IT'S HARD TO GET THROUGH... I'D HOPED TO MEET UP WITH TODOROKI AND YAOYOROZU, BUT AT THIS RATE...
LET'S JUST KEEP MOVING.
WE GOTTA LET THE PROS KNOW THAT BAKUGO'S WITH US.
YEAH...
NOW IT'S...

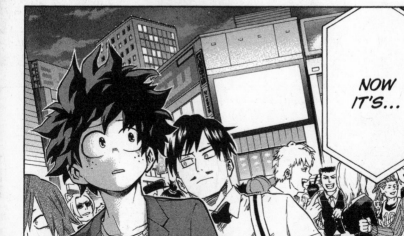

POLICE
DO NOT ENTER
...YOUR TURN!

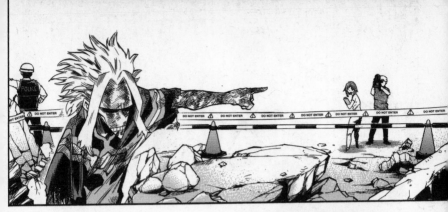

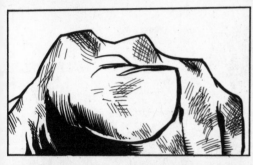

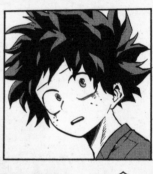

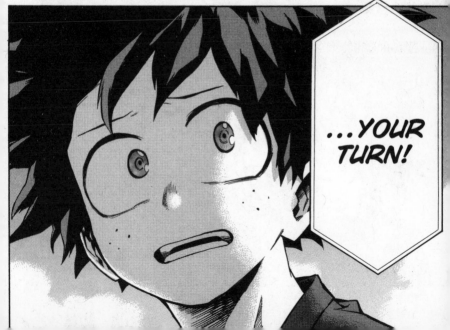

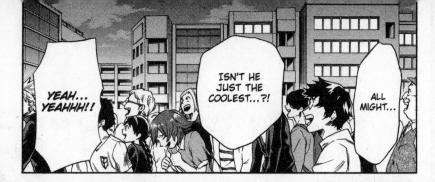

ALL MIGHT...
ISN'T HE JUST THE COOLEST...?!
YEAH... YEAHHH!!
TO THE CASUAL LISTENER, THAT BRIEF MESSAGE...
...SEEMED LIKE A WARNING DIRECTED AT OTHER CRIMINALS STILL OUT THERE...
...TELLING THEM THE SYMBOL OF PEACE HADN'T BEEN BROKEN...
BUT FOR ME, IT MEANT THE EXACT OPPOSITE.

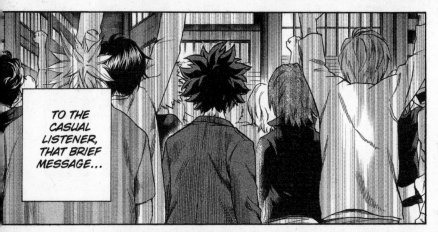

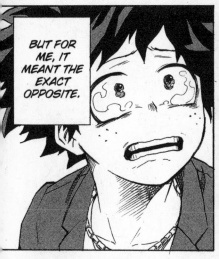

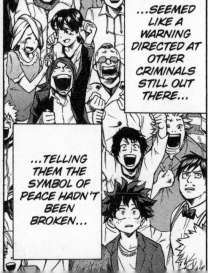

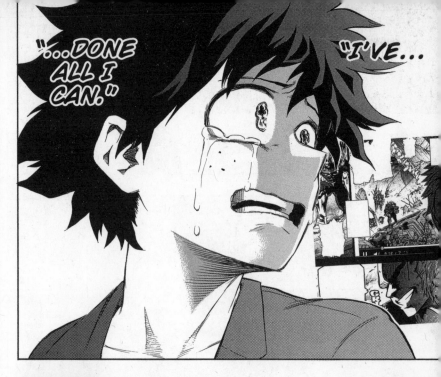

"I'VE...

"...DONE ALL I CAN."

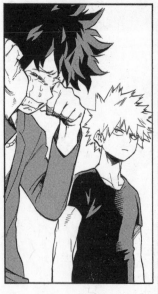

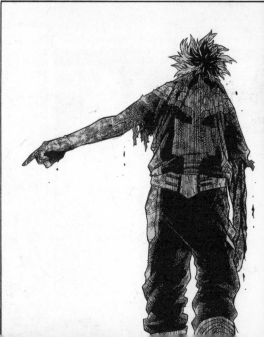

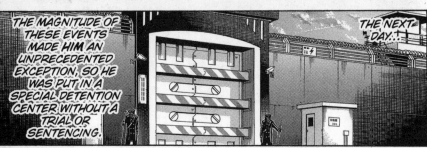

THE NEXT DAY...
THE MAGNITUDE OF THESE EVENTS MADE HIM AN UNPRECEDENTED EXCEPTION, SO HE WAS PUT IN A SPECIAL DETENTION CENTER WITHOUT A TRIAL OR SENTENCING.
WHERE AM I?
SKWEEK
SKWEEK
SHUT YOUR MOUTH!! IT SHOULD BE OBVIOUS WHERE YOU ARE!!
YOU'D BE GETTING OFF EASY IF THEY GAVE YOU THE DEATH PENALTY! THIS PLACE IS WHERE YOUR KIND OF SCUM GETS LOCKED UP!!
AHH... A PRISON, THEN... I COULDN'T TELL.
THERE ARE...FAR TOO MANY SENSORS...
SQUEAK
...? WHAT'D YOU SAY?
SPEAK UP...

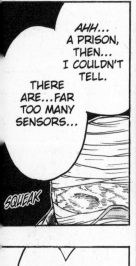

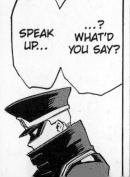

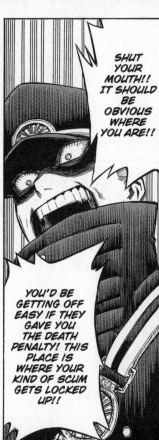

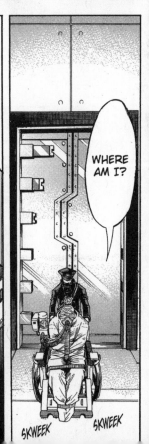

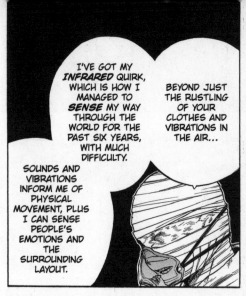

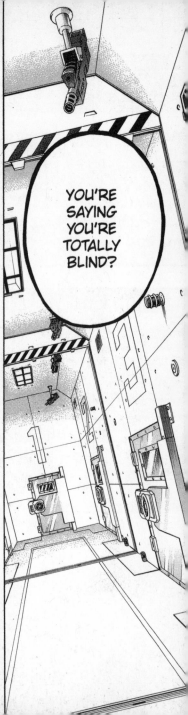

YOU'RE SAYING YOU'RE TOTALLY BLIND?
BEYOND JUST THE RUSTLING OF YOUR CLOTHES AND VIBRATIONS IN THE AIR...
I'VE GOT MY INFRARED QUIRK, WHICH IS HOW I MANAGED TO SENSE MY WAY THROUGH THE WORLD FOR THE PAST SIX YEARS, WITH MUCH DIFFICULTY.
SOUNDS AND VIBRATIONS INFORM ME OF PHYSICAL MOVEMENT, PLUS I CAN SENSE PEOPLE'S EMOTIONS AND THE SURROUNDING LAYOUT.
BUT THESE SENSORS RENDER MY SENSING ABILITIES ALL BUT USELESS. WHAT A SHAME...
HUMM
NO WAY... HE FOUGHT ALL MIGHT...
...IN THIS DECREPIT STATE...?!

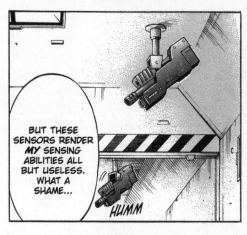

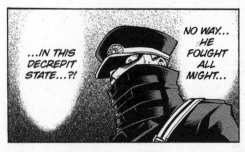

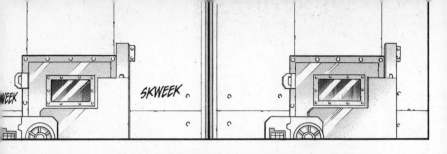

SKWEEK
I LOST, ALL MIGHT.
AND WHAT A PATHETIC STRUGGLE I PUT UP.
BUT YOU WERE WRONG.
AT THE END OF OUR BATTLE, YOU LEFT THE FUTURE IN YOUR PUPIL'S HANDS.

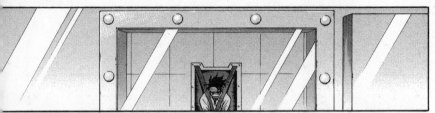

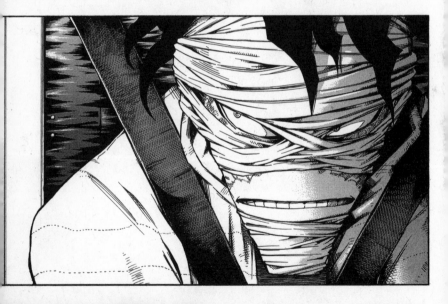

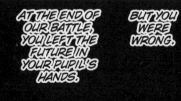

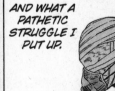

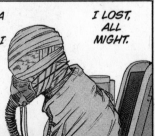

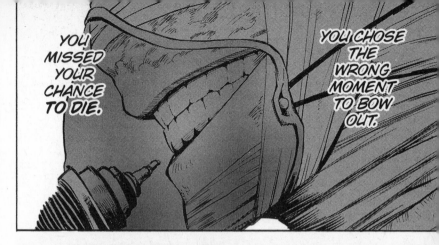

YOU CHOSE THE WRONG MOMENT TO BOW OUT.
YOU MISSED YOUR CHANCE TO DIE.
A TEACHER'S JOB...
...IS TO RAISE THEIR WARDS TO BE INDEPENDENT.
HE RELIED ON HIS TEACHER, AND NOW YOU'VE LOCKED ME UP, FAR OUT OF HIS REACH.
ALL YOU'VE DONE IS STOKED HIS RAGE, AND NOW HE'S READY TO TAKE CHARGE. HE HAS ALLIES. HE'S LEARNED HOW TO RECRUIT MORE.
YOU'LL BE FINE, TOMURA SHIGARAKI.
YOUR EXPERIENCES, YOUR HATRED, YOUR REGRETS...
USE THEM TO FUEL YOURSELF.

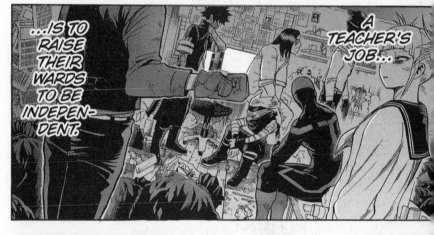

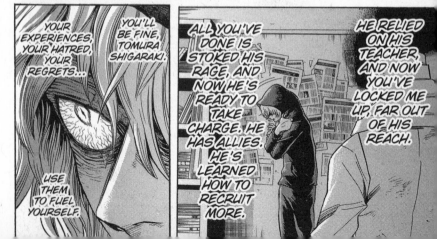

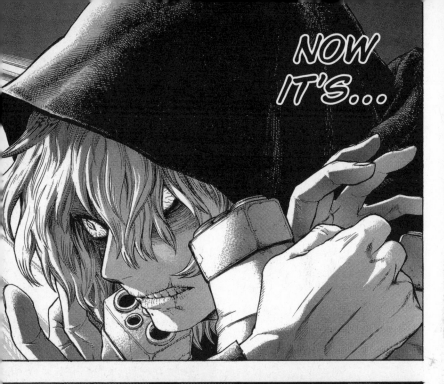

NOW IT'S...

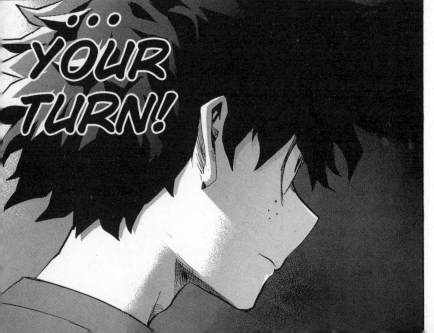

...YOUR TURN!

# PARENT

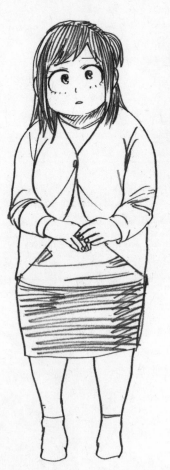

**Birthday: 7/4**
**Height: 160 cm**
**Favorite Thing: Izuku**

### THE MOM

Her husband is working overseas, so she's raised Izuku alone, for the most part. She's not very plucky, and she tends to be reserved. The concern and guilt she felt regarding Izuku led her to put on some weight.

I always feel really sorry when drawing her for some reason.

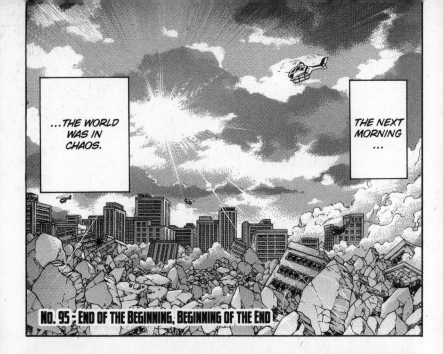

THE NEXT MORNING...
...THE WORLD WAS IN CHAOS.
No. 95 - End of the Beginning, Beginning of the End
NEW
HALF OF KAMINO WARD DESTROYED
KAMINO WARD
ALL MIGHT'S TRUE FORM
THE CAPTURED NOMU ARE THE SAME AS THE OTHERS.
THEY DON'T REACT TO STIMULI LIKE ORDINARY HUMANS, AND WE'VE GATHERED NO NEW INFORMATION FROM THEM.
THE WAREHOUSE THEY WERE BEING STORED IN WAS COMPLETELY DESTROYED.
AT THIS POINT, WE CAN ONLY CONTINUE TO INVESTIGATE THE METHODS BY WHICH THEY'RE CREATED.

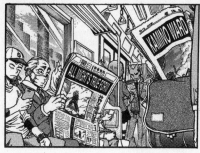

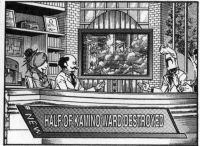

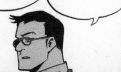

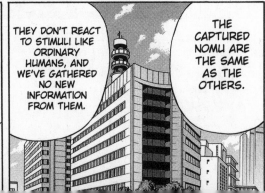

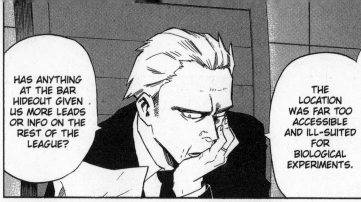

BUT THAT WAREHOUSE WAS A DECOY ALL ALONG, WASN'T IT?
THE LOCATION WAS FAR TOO ACCESSIBLE AND ILL-SUITED FOR BIOLOGICAL EXPERIMENTS.
HAS ANYTHING AT THE BAR HIDEOUT GIVEN US MORE LEADS OR INFO ON THE REST OF THE LEAGUE?
WE'RE STILL INVESTIGATING.
HMM ...
THOUGH THE RINGLEADER IS IN CUSTODY ...
...SHIGARAKI AND THE OTHER PERPETRATORS ARE STILL OUT THERE.
IF WE'RE BEING GENEROUS, HERE...WE COULD CALL IT A DRAW.
YOU FOOL.
WE LOST THE SYMBOL OF PEACE... AND FOR WHAT?!

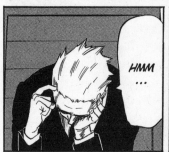

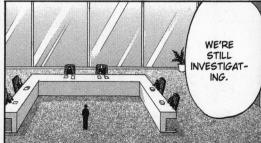

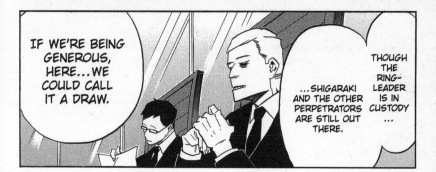

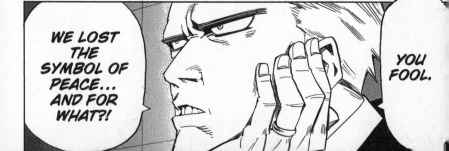

THE WORLD NOW KNOWS OF ALL MIGHT'S WEAKENED STATE.
THE INDOMITABLE SYMBOL OF PEACE AS WE KNEW HIM IS GONE.
THE PEOPLE OF THIS COUNTRY KNOW IT.
THE VILLAINS KNOW IT TOO.
THAT'S THE PRICE WE PAY FOR ALWAYS RELYING ON ONE MAN...
TO THINK THAT YOU CAN GET THIS FAR AS LONG AS YOU GATHER ENOUGH FOOLS... AND NOW EVERYONE KNOWS THAT.
THAT'S WHAT REALLY WORRIES ME.
INITIAL PROFILING PAINTED TOMURA SHIGARAKI AS A MAN WITH A CHILDISH DISPOSITION.
BUT EACH DASTARDLY PLAN THAT HE COOKS UP AS THEIR LEADER BECOMES MORE AND MORE INTRICATE...
HE'S COMPLETELY FOCUSED ON THE EFFECT HE CAN HAVE ON SOCIETY AS A WHOLE.

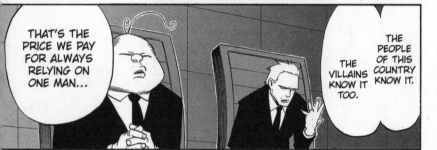

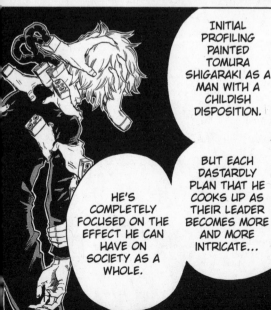

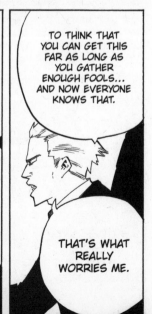

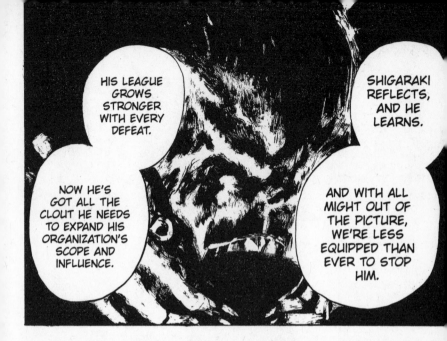

SHIGARAKI REFLECTS, AND HE LEARNS.
HIS LEAGUE GROWS STRONGER WITH EVERY DEFEAT.
NOW HE'S GOT ALL THE CLOUT HE NEEDS TO EXPAND HIS ORGANIZATION'S SCOPE AND INFLUENCE.
AND WITH ALL MIGHT OUT OF THE PICTURE, WE'RE LESS EQUIPPED THAN EVER TO STOP HIM.
DID WE TIP OUR HAND? ARE WE SECOND-GUESSING OURSELVES?
AND GETTING CAUGHT UP ON THE NEGATIVES HERE?
NOT SURE.
WHAT WE CAN SAY FOR CERTAIN IS THIS... WE *HAVE* TO CAPTURE THEM.
AS THE POLICE...
...WE HAVE TO PROVE THAT WE CAN DO MORE THAN JUST SIMPLY TAKING IN THE VILLAINS THAT THE HEROES DEFEAT.
WE NEED TO MAKE SOME CHANGES.

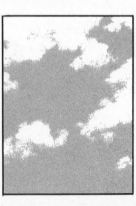

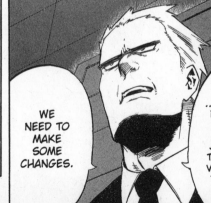

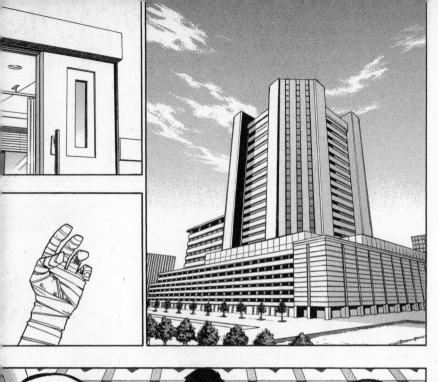

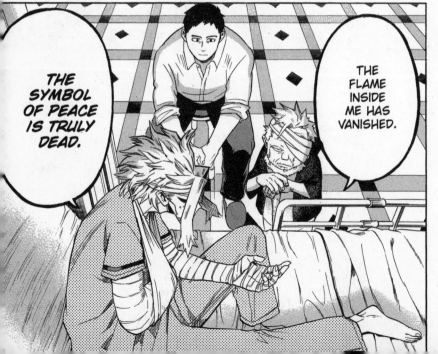

THE FLAME INSIDE ME HAS VANISHED.
THE SYMBOL OF PEACE IS TRULY DEAD.

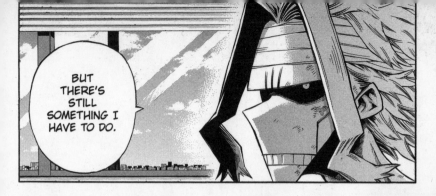

BUT THERE'S STILL SOMETHING I HAVE TO DO.
SO TOMURA SHIGARAKI ...
...IS SHIMURA'S GRANDSON ...?
DON'T FORGET WHO TOLD US THAT THOUGH. SHOULDN'T WE TAKE IT WITH A GRAIN OF SALT?
DIDN'T THE TWO OF YOU EVER INTERACT WITH MS. SHIMURA'S FAMILY?
WELL...
SHIMURA'S HUSBAND WAS KILLED.

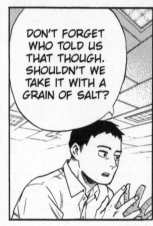

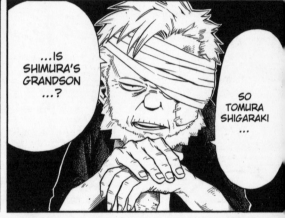

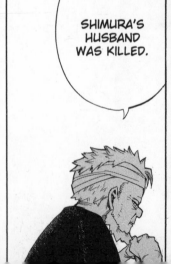

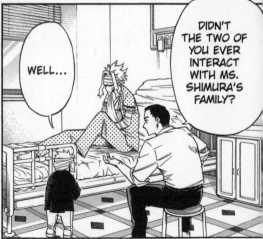

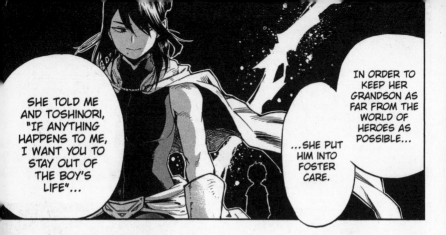

IN ORDER TO KEEP HER GRANDSON AS FAR FROM THE WORLD OF HEROES AS POSSIBLE...
...SHE PUT HIM INTO FOSTER CARE.
SHE TOLD ME AND TOSHINORI, "IF ANYTHING HAPPENS TO ME, I WANT YOU TO STAY OUT OF THE BOY'S LIFE"...
SO THAT PROMISE WAS TURNED ON ITS HEAD...
PRETTY TRAGIC.
TO THINK, MY MASTER'S OWN KIN LOST HIMSELF IN SO MUCH EVIL...
I HAVE TO FIND SHIGARAKI... I'LL FIND HIM AND...
NO.
FIND HIM AND WHAT?
IF YOU THINK HE'S ANYTHING LESS THAN A VILLAIN, NO GOOD CAN COME OF IT.
NO MATTER WHO HIS PARENTS ARE, HE'S STILL A DANGEROUS CRIMINAL.

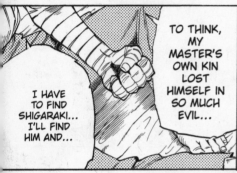

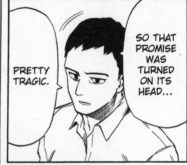

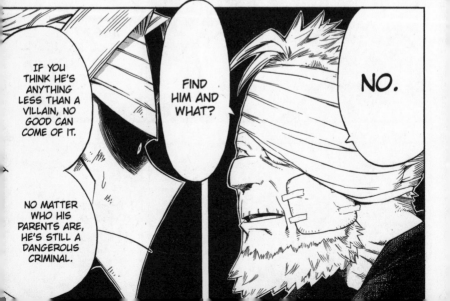

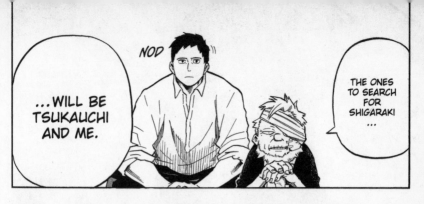

THE ONES TO SEARCH FOR SHIGARAKI ...
NOD
...WILL BE TSUKAUCHI AND ME.
YOU STAY AT U.A. AND DO WHAT NEEDS TO BE DONE.
EVEN IF YOU'RE NO LONGER THE SYMBOL OF PEACE...
...ALL MIGHT IS STILL ALIVE AND WITH US.
AFTER THAT, WE RECONVENED WITH TODOROKI AND THE OTHERS.
KACCHAN WENT WITH THE POLICE.

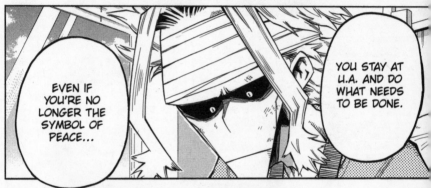

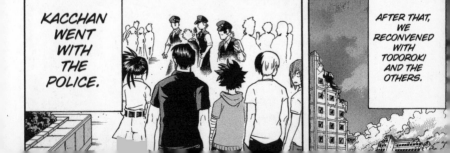

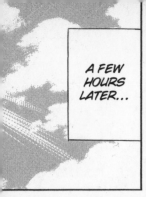

KACCHAN ...
...WAS QUIET.
A FEW HOURS LATER...
...WE WERE ON OUR WAY HOME.
GOOD-BYE, THEN.
THANKS A LOT, YOU GUYS.
YOU THREE! BE SURE TO GO STRAIGHT HOME!
THANKS FOR EVERYTHING!
RIGHT... SEE YOU GUYS AT SCHOOL.

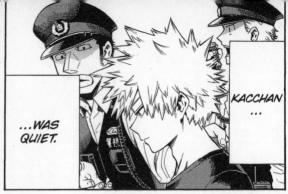

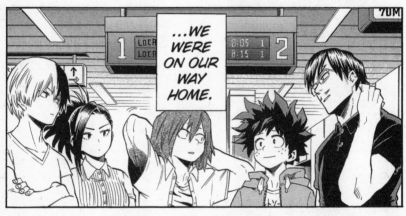

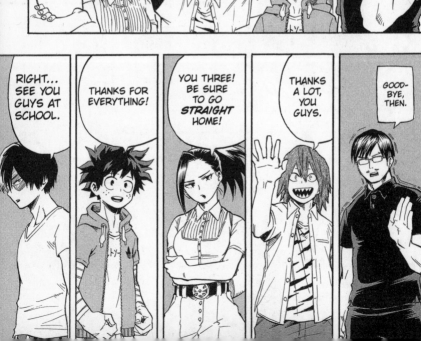

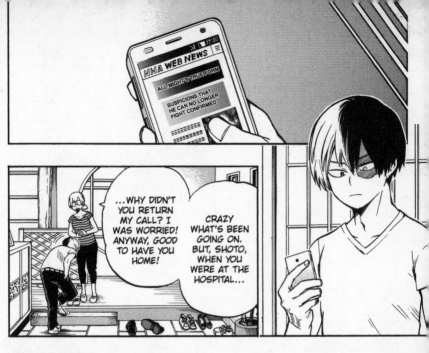

NHA WEB NEWS
ALL MIGHT'S TRUE FORM
SUSPICIONS THAT HE CAN NO LONGER FIGHT CONFIRMED
CRAZY WHAT'S BEEN GOING ON. BUT, SHOTO, WHEN YOU WERE AT THE HOSPITAL...
...WHY DIDN'T YOU RETURN MY CALL? I WAS WORRIED! ANYWAY, GOOD TO HAVE YOU HOME!
SORRY, SIS...
KER-SLAM
KERSLAM
HE GOT BACK A LITTLE WHILE AGO. BEEN GOING AT IT LIKE THAT, SINCE...

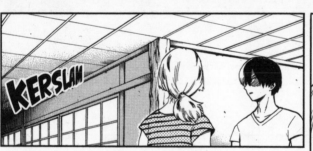

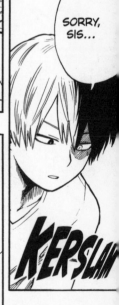

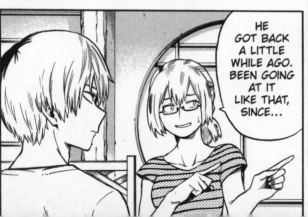

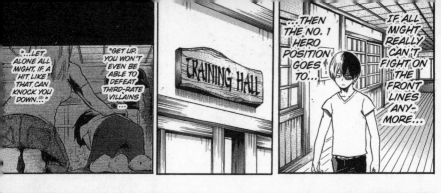

IF ALL MIGHT REALLY CAN'T FIGHT ON THE FRONT LINES ANYMORE...
...THEN THE NO. 1 HERO POSITION GOES TO...
TRAINING HALL
"GET UP. YOU WON'T EVEN BE ABLE TO DEFEAT THIRD-RATE VILLAINS...
"...LET ALONE ALL MIGHT, IF A HIT LIKE THAT CAN KNOCK YOU DOWN..."
HAHH... HAHH...
I CAN'T ACCEPT THIS...
WHO COULD? CAN'T ACCEPT IT.
I JUST CAN'T!

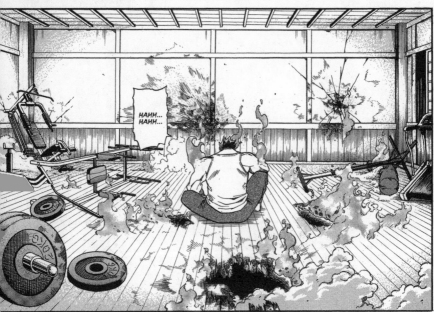

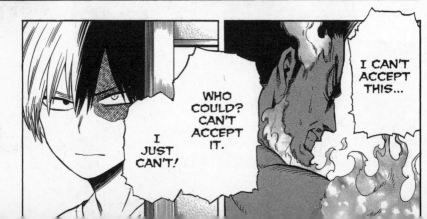

LOOKED LIKE... ALL MIGHT WAS IN REAL TROUBLE. AND YOU HAD A HARD TIME GETTING HOME, IZUKU?

WELCOME BACK.

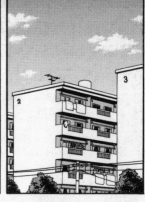

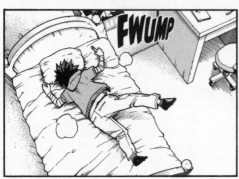

FWUMP

YEAH...

ALL MIGHT...

WHAT'S GOING TO HAPPEN NEXT? DID I REALLY DO THE RIGHT THING?

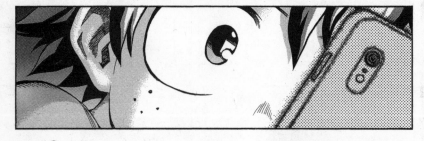

BZZ

BZZ

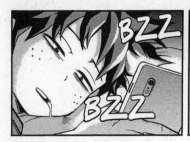

BZZ

BZZ

BZZ

BZZ

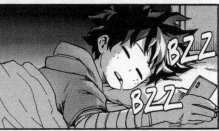

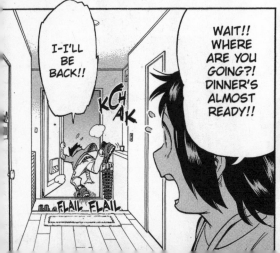

I-I'LL BE BACK!!

WAIT!! WHERE ARE YOU GOING?! DINNER'S ALMOST READY!!

KCH AK

FLAIL FLAIL

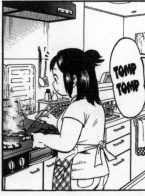

TOMP TOMP

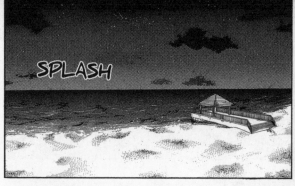

SPLASH

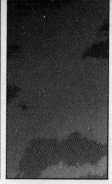

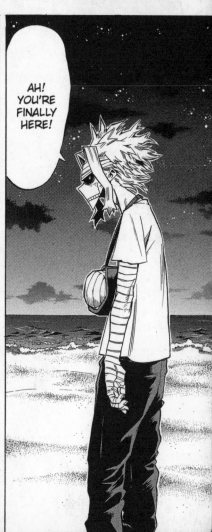

AH! YOU'RE FINALLY HERE!

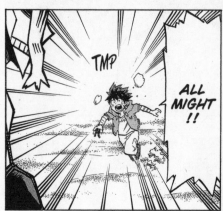

TMP

ALL MIGHT !!

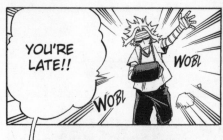

YOU'RE LATE!!

WOBL

WOBL

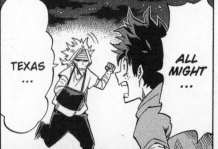

TEXAS ...

ALL MIGHT ...

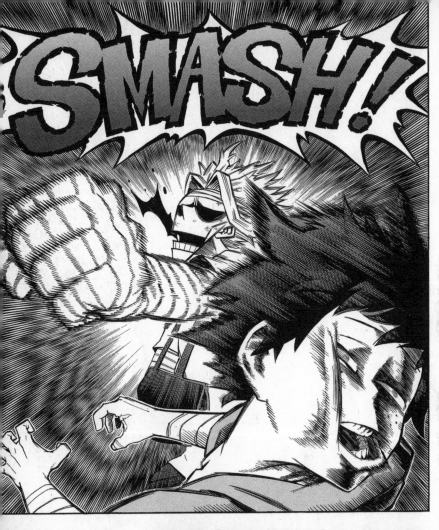

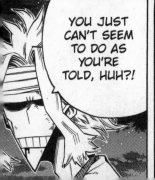

YOU JUST CAN'T SEEM TO DO AS YOU'RE TOLD, HUH?!

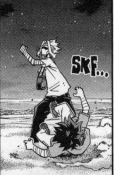

SKF...

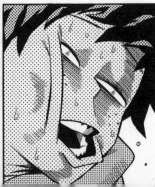

IT WAS ALMOST ALL FOR NOTHING.
YOU'RE JUST AS RECKLESS AS...
...
MIDORIYA, KID, I'M...
I'M OFFICIALLY RETIRED, NOW. I CAN'T FIGHT ANYMORE. NOT LIKE THIS.
FWOOM
?!

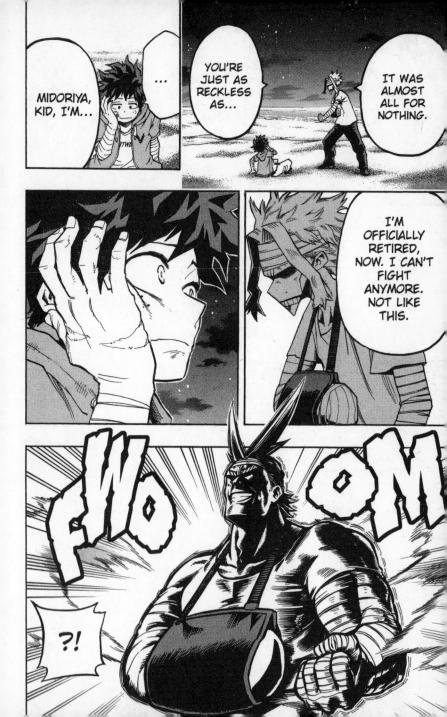

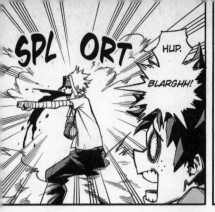

HUP.
HUP.
HUP.
HUP.
SPL ORT
BLARGHH!
THE EMBER OF ONE FOR ALL IS GONE...
AND I CAN'T MAINTAIN MY MUSCULAR FORM AT ALL...
AND AT THE END OF THE DAY, YOU STILL...
...RUN HEADLONG INTO DANGER EVERY SINGLE TIME!
DESPITE ALL OUR WARNINGS, YOU STILL GO AND GET ALL BEAT UP!
BUT THIS TIME ...!
FW IP

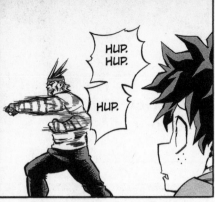

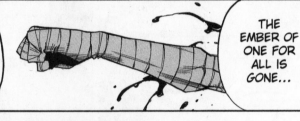

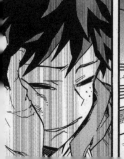

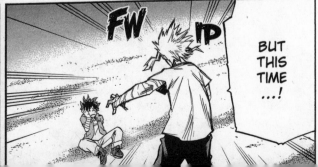

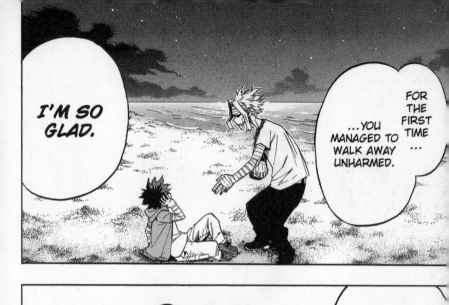

FOR THE FIRST TIME ...
...YOU MANAGED TO WALK AWAY UNHARMED.
I'M SO GLAD.
FROM NOW ON, I CAN FOCUS ON RAISING YOU RIGHT.
SHP
EVEN THOUGH I'VE BEEN REDUCED TO THIS STATE... LET'S DO OUR BEST, OKAY?
UGHH ...
ALL...
ALL MIGHT, I...

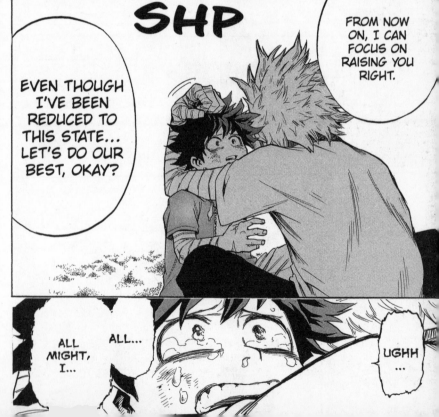

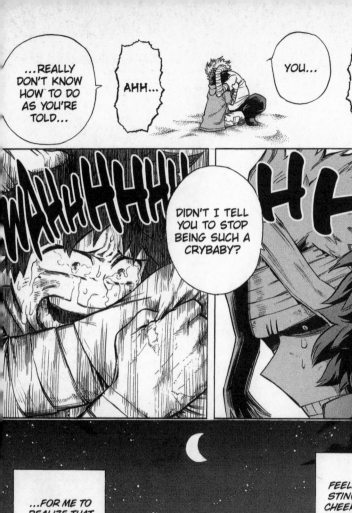

UGH...
YOU...
AHH...
...REALLY DON'T KNOW HOW TO DO AS YOU'RE TOLD...
DIDN'T I TELL YOU TO STOP BEING SUCH A CRYBABY?
WAHHHHHHHHHH
FEELING THE STING ON MY CHEEKS...WAS MORE THAN ENOUGH...
...FOR ME TO REALIZE THAT THE SUN HAD SET ON THE ERA OF ALL MIGHT.

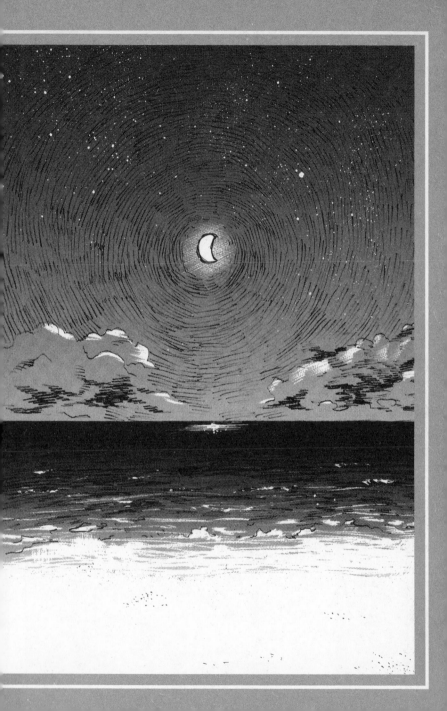

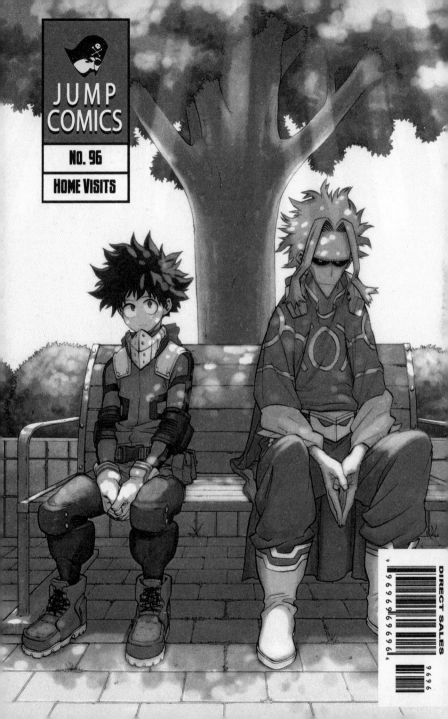

JUMP
COMICS

NO. 96

HOME VISITS

MY HERO
ACADEMIA

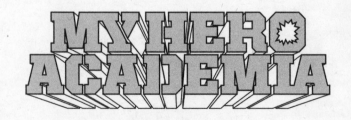

IT'S THE HERO BILLBOARD CHART JP!
THE BIANNUAL RANKING OF CURRENT HEROES, BASED ON...
...MISSION COMPLETION RATE, CONTRIBUTIONS TO SOCIETY AND PUBLIC SUPPORT!!
WHO COULD HAVE PREDICTED THIS HAPPENING TO THE NO. 1 UNBEATABLE HERO?! AND IT'S NOT JUST JAPAN. AMERICA, THE HOME OF HEROES, IS IN AN UPROAR!
WE'VE NOW SEEN ALL MIGHT'S TRUE FORM. HE'S REACHED HIS LIMIT!
IN LIGHT OF THIS, HE RECENTLY ANNOUNCED HIS RETIREMENT FROM THE WORLD OF HEROES!!
ALSO, REGARDING THE NO. 4 HERO, BEST JEANIST...
シーニアス
OFFICE
GENIUS
THOUGH HE MANAGED TO SURVIVE THE RECENT INCIDENT, HE'LL BE OUT FOR A LONG WHILE!!
ALSO, REGARDING THE NO. 32 HERO, RAGDOLL OF THE SUPER-POPULAR PUSSYCATS...
SHE'S BEEN UNABLE TO USE HER QUIRK EVER SINCE HER ABDUCTION, SO SHE'LL BE TAKING AN INDEFINITE LEAVE.

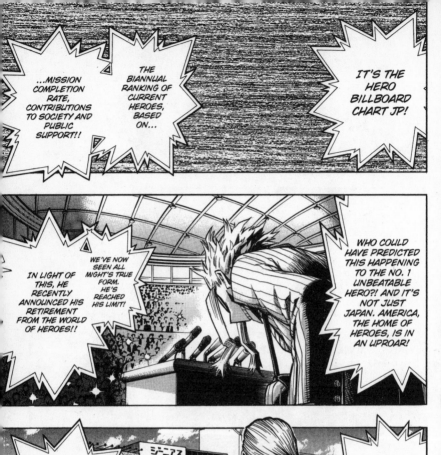

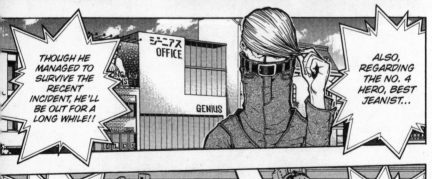

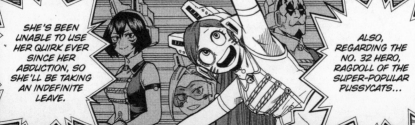

A GREAT NUMBER OF HEROES HAVE HAD THEIR LIVES SUDDENLY AFFECTED IN THE EVENT WE NOW KNOW AS THE **KAMINO NIGHTMARE**!!
WHAT WILL BECOME OF JAPAN AND ITS HEROES? THAT'S ALL FOR TODAY'S NEWS!
NEXT UP IS THE WEATHER ...
...WITH MR. KIHARA!
YOUR SACRIFICE SAVED COUNTLESS LIVES.
THE PEOPLE, THE HEROES AND I, THE PRINCIPAL, CANNOT POSSIBLY THANK YOU ENOUGH.

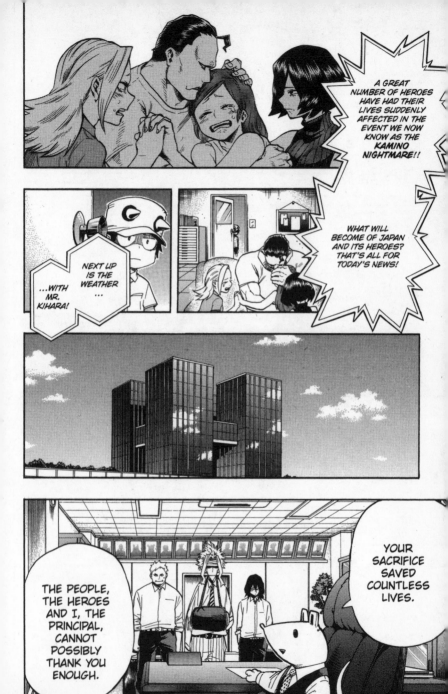

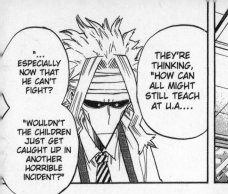

HOWEVER, CONCERNING YOUR CURRENT TENURE AS A TEACHER HERE AT U.A....
THERE'S BEEN A FAIR AMOUNT OF CRITICISM COMING FROM THE PUBLIC.
THEY'RE THINKING, "HOW CAN ALL MIGHT STILL TEACH AT U.A....
"...ESPECIALLY NOW THAT HE CAN'T FIGHT?
"WOULDN'T THE CHILDREN JUST GET CAUGHT UP IN ANOTHER HORRIBLE INCIDENT?"
THEY'RE ALL JUST UNEASY...
...WHICH IS WHY WE HAVE TO COME TOGETHER AND GET STRONGER.
WE NEED TO HOLD ON TO THE PUBLIC'S TRUST IN HEROES THAT *YOU* WORKED SO HARD TO BUILD.
THE WHOLE INCIDENT SHOULD BE ENOUGH TO MAKE EVERYONE REALIZE...
WE'VE BEEN PLACING THE ENTIRE BURDEN ON YOU ALL THIS TIME...
...AND IT'S BEEN A HEAVY ONE.
THERE ARE STILL THREATS OUT THERE...
WE NEED TO MAKE SURE OUR STUDENTS ARE IN A SAFE, STABLE ENVIRONMENT.
TO THAT END, WE'LL BE IMPLEMENTING A PLAN I'VE BEEN RUMINATING ON FOR QUITE SOME TIME.
VLAD AND I WILL HANDLE CLASS B, WITH ITS MANY CASUALTIES ...
ALL MIGHT AND ERASER HEAD WILL DEAL WITH CLASS A...

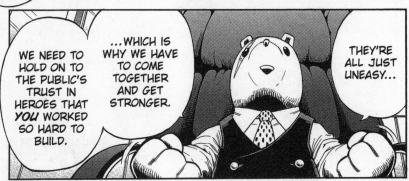

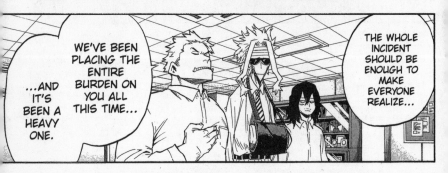

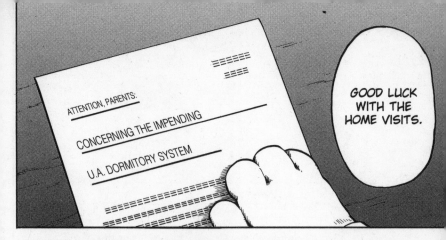

GOOD LUCK WITH THE HOME VISITS.
ATTENTION, PARENTS:
CONCERNING THE IMPENDING
U.A. DORMITORY SYSTEM
HM... THIS DOESN'T SOUND LIKE MUSIC TO MY EARS...
JIRO
SHE MAY BE GETTING BETTER, BUT MY ONLY DAUGHTER STILL GOT HURT.
NOW YOU'RE TALKING ABOUT DORMS, LIKE NOTHING EVEN HAPPENED?
I ASSURE YOU THAT WE'RE TAKING YOUR FEELINGS ON THE MATTER TO HEART, MR. JIRO, BUT...
WE NOW REALIZE THAT WE WERE OVERCONFIDENT. WE TOOK THESE THREATS TOO LIGHTLY, SO WE NEED TO SERIOUSLY REEXAMINE OUR POLICIES.
WILL YOU PLEASE TRUST US WITH THIS?
BOW
I'VE NO DOUBT THAT WE CAN STILL HELP KYOKA BECOME THE GREAT HERO SHE'S MEANT TO BE...

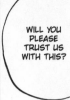

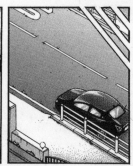

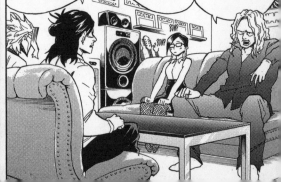

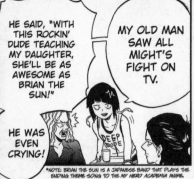

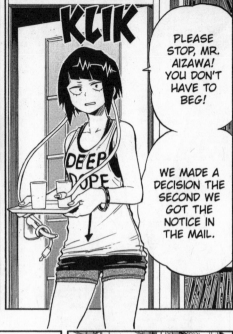

KLIK
PLEASE STOP, MR. AIZAWA! YOU DON'T HAVE TO BEG!
WE MADE A DECISION THE SECOND WE GOT THE NOTICE IN THE MAIL.
MY OLD MAN SAW ALL MIGHT'S FIGHT ON TV.
HE SAID, "WITH THIS ROCKIN' DUDE TEACHING MY DAUGHTER, SHE'LL BE AS AWESOME AS BRIAN THE SUN!"
HE WAS EVEN CRYING!
*NOTE: BRIAN THE SUN IS A JAPANESE BAND THAT PLAYS THE ENDING THEME SONG TO THE MY HERO ACADEMIA ANIME.
WHAT THE HECK, KYOKA?! YOUR OLD MAN'S JUST TRYIN' TO LOOK LIKE A GOOD, CONCERNED PARENT HERE!!
OH, STUFF IT, POPS.
THAT'S ENOUGH, YOU TWO! THIS AIN'T NO PUNK HOUSEHOLD.
I WAS READY FOR A MUCH HARSHER RECEPTION...
...
I SHOULD BUY YOU TO A DRINK.
HA HA HA...
KNOCK IT OFF. THAT'S NOT LIKE YOU AT ALL.
BESIDES, I CAN'T DRINK.
LET'S GO TO THE NEXT HOUSE.

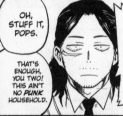

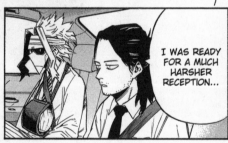

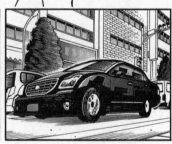

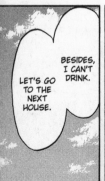

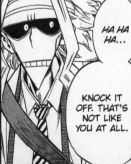

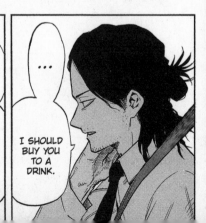

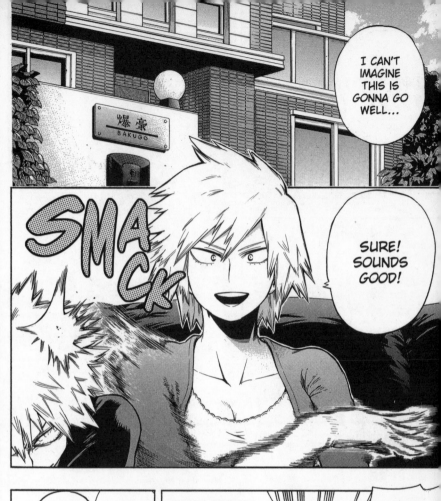

爆豪
BAKUGO
I CAN'T IMAGINE THIS IS GONNA GO WELL...
SURE! SOUNDS GOOD!
SMACK
STOP SMACKING ME, YOU HAG. I'LL SEND YOU FLYING!!
SMACK
THAT'S ENOUGH OUTTA YOU!! WE WOULDN'T BE IN THIS MESS IF YOU HADN'T BEEN SO WEAK AND GOTTEN CAUGHT IN THE FIRST PLACE!!
COME ON, YOU TWO... C-CUT IT OUT...
THE TEACHERS MUST BE SHOCKED BY ALL THIS...

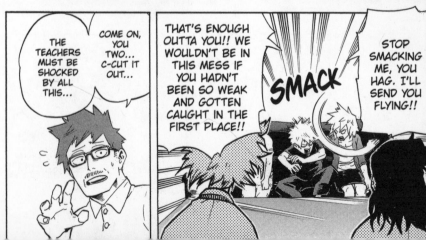

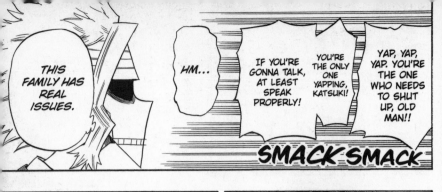

THIS FAMILY HAS REAL ISSUES.

HM...

IF YOU'RE GONNA TALK, AT LEAST SPEAK PROPERLY!

YOU'RE THE ONLY ONE YAPPING, KATSUKI!

YAP, YAP, YAP. YOU'RE THE ONE WHO NEEDS TO SHUT UP, OLD MAN!!

SMACK SMACK

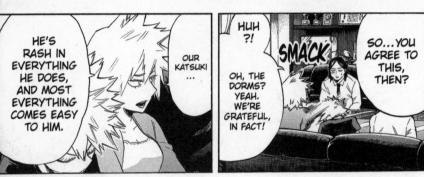

HE'S RASH IN EVERYTHING HE DOES, AND MOST EVERYTHING COMES EASY TO HIM.

OUR KATSUKI...

HUH ?!

OH, THE DORMS? YEAH. WE'RE GRATEFUL, IN FACT!

SMACK

SO...YOU AGREE TO THIS, THEN?

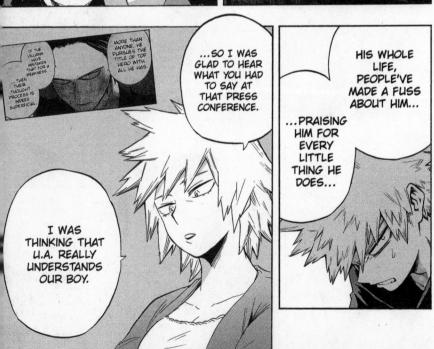

IF THE VILLAINS HAVE MISTAKEN THAT FOR A WEAKNESS...

...THEN THEIR THOUGHT PROCESS IS INDEED SUPERFICIAL.

MORE THAN ANYONE, HE PURSUES THE TITLE OF TOP HERO WITH ALL HE HAS.

...SO I WAS GLAD TO HEAR WHAT YOU HAD TO SAY AT THAT PRESS CONFERENCE.

HIS WHOLE LIFE, PEOPLE'VE MADE A FUSS ABOUT HIM...

...PRAISING HIM FOR EVERY LITTLE THING HE DOES...

I WAS THINKING THAT U.A. REALLY UNDERSTANDS OUR BOY.

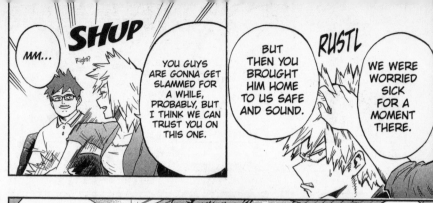

MM...

Right?

**SHUP**

YOU GUYS ARE GONNA GET SLAMMED FOR A WHILE, PROBABLY, BUT I THINK WE CAN TRUST YOU ON THIS ONE.

BUT THEN YOU BROUGHT HIM HOME TO US SAFE AND SOUND.

**RUSTL**

WE WERE WORRIED SICK FOR A MOMENT THERE.

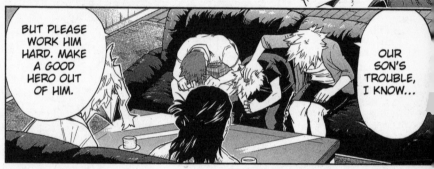

BUT PLEASE WORK HIM HARD. MAKE A GOOD HERO OUT OF HIM.

OUR SON'S TROUBLE, I KNOW...

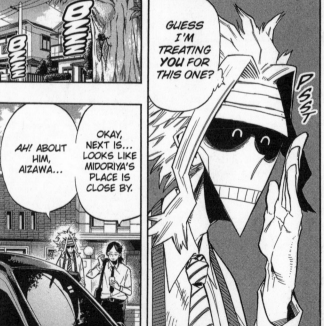

**BZZZ**

**BZZZ**

GUESS I'M TREATING YOU FOR THIS ONE?

**PSST**

AH! ABOUT HIM, AIZAWA...

OKAY, NEXT IS... LOOKS LIKE MIDORIYA'S PLACE IS CLOSE BY.

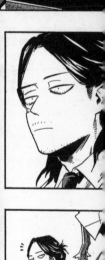

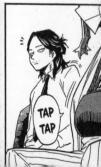

**TAP TAP**

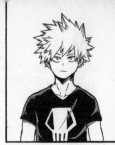

HM?

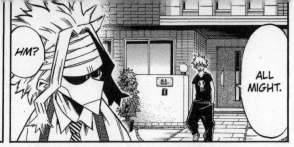

ALL MIGHT.

WHAT IS HE TO YOU?

DEKU...

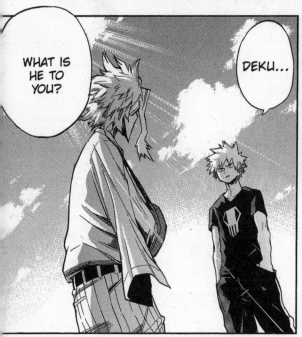

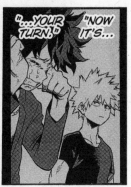

"...YOUR TURN."

"NOW IT'S..."

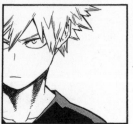

I'M SORRY, BAKUGO, KID.

MY STUDENT...

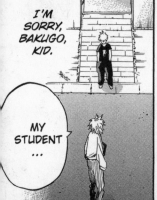

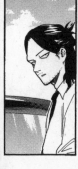

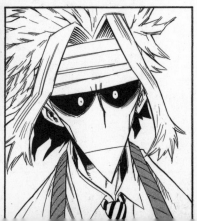

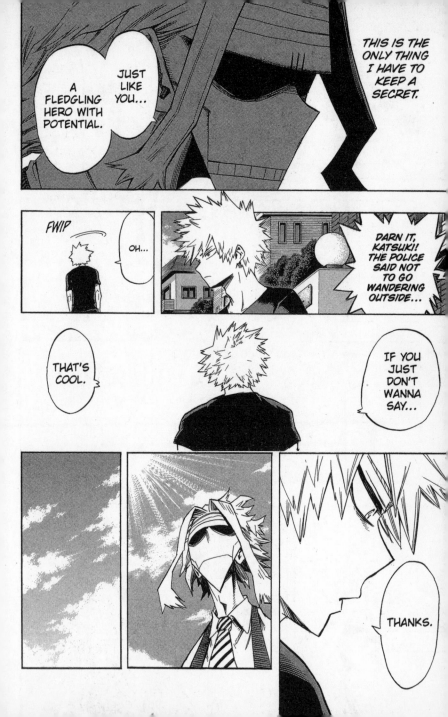

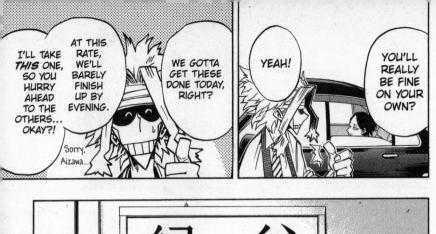

YOU'LL REALLY BE FINE ON YOUR OWN?
YEAH!
WE GOTTA GET THESE DONE TODAY, RIGHT?
AT THIS RATE, WE'LL BARELY FINISH UP BY EVENING.
I'LL TAKE *THIS* ONE, SO YOU HURRY AHEAD TO THE OTHERS... OKAY?!
Sorry, Aizawa...
緑谷
*SIGN: MIDORIYA
BADUM BADUM
OH...
P-PL...
BADUM
BADUM
PLEASE COME IN!
DRESS SHIRT
IZUKU
ALLMIGHT
ALLMIGHT

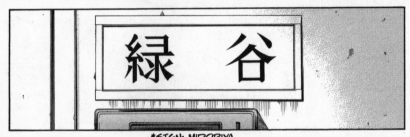

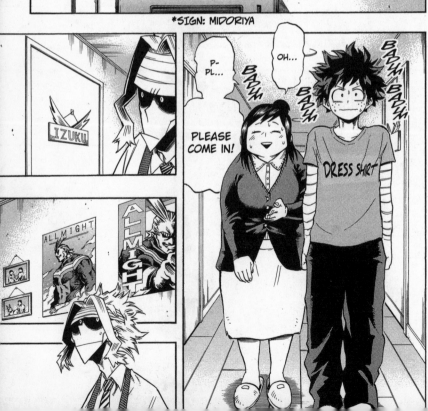

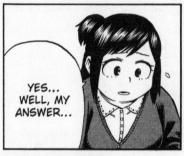

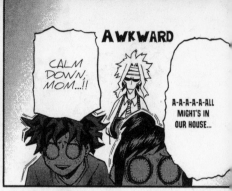

A-A-A-A-A-ALL MIGHT'S IN OUR HOUSE...
AWKWARD
CALM DOWN, MOM...!!
WE WERE HOPING TO GET THE WORD OUT AHEAD OF TIME...
...WITH REGARD TO U.A.'S NEW DORMITORY SYSTEM...
YES... WELL, MY ANSWER...
...IS...
...NO.
DRESS SHIRT
DRESS SHIRT

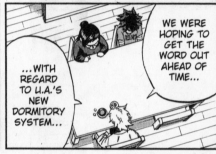

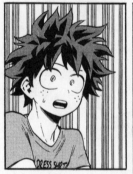

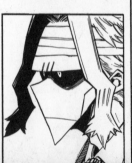

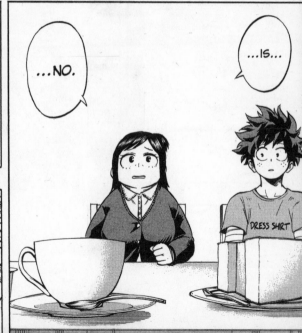

BUT, MOM?! YOU SAID IT WAS OKAY YESTERDAY...
I'VE BEEN THINKING ABOUT IT, AND NOW I'M NOT SO SURE.
IZUKU USED TO BE QUIRKLESS...
...BUT HE STILL GREW UP ADMIRING YOU.
AND EVER SINCE HE SOMEHOW DEVELOPED A QUIRK...
...AND ENROLLED AT U.A....
...MY IZUKU...
...IS ALWAYS GETTING HURT.
HIS ARM.
YOU KNOW ABOUT IT, RIGHT?
DRESS SHIRT
IF HE INJURES IT AGAIN, HE MIGHT LOSE IT FOREVER...!
OF COURSE I SAW YOUR FIGHT ON TV THE OTHER DAY.
AS A CITIZEN, I'M BEYOND GRATEFUL FOR WHAT YOU'VE DONE.
BUT... AS A PARENT, IT SCARED ME.
IZUKU...
...LOOKS UP TO YOU.

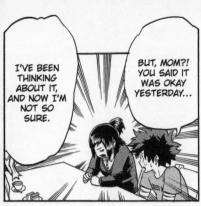

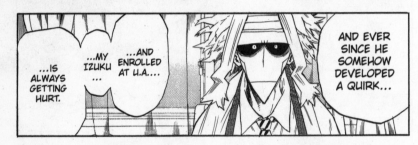

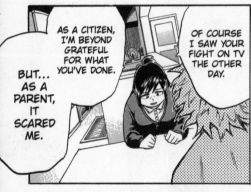

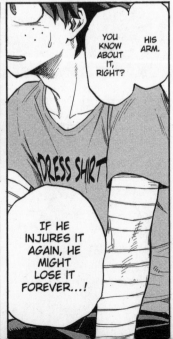

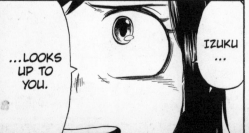

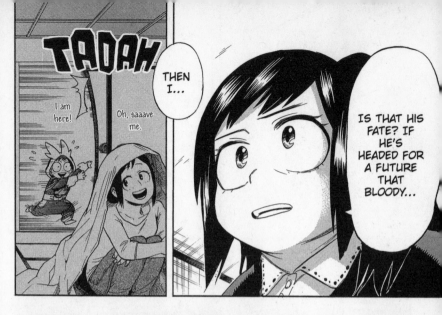

IS THAT HIS FATE? IF HE'S HEADED FOR A FUTURE THAT BLOODY...
THEN I...
TADAH
Oh, saaave me.
I am here!
I'M SORRY, IZUKU. I'M SORRY ...!!
I...
BACK WHEN HE WAS QUIRKLESS...
...HE GOT SO MUCH JOY FROM WATCHING HEROES DO THEIR WORK.
SO NOW I'M THINKING... SHOULDN'T THAT BE GOOD ENOUGH?

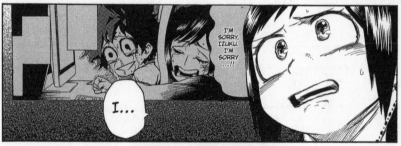

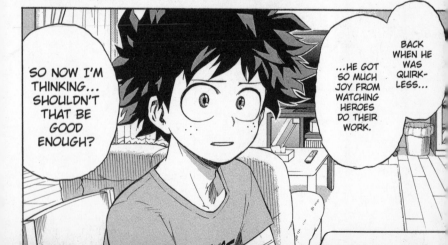

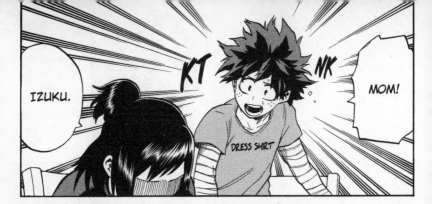

MOM!
KT NK
DRESS SHIRT
IZUKU.
I'LL ALWAYS SUPPORT YOU...
...BUT THAT DOESN'T MEAN I DON'T WORRY.
I NEED ANOTHER WAY. MY OWN WAY...
...SO THAT NO ONE HAS TO WORRY ABOUT ME.
YOU KNOW THAT.
IT WAS ALMOST ALL FOR NOTHING.
I KNOW IZUKU WANTS TO KEEP GOING TO U.A.
BUT...
DO YOU REALLY...
...HAVE TO GO BACK TO U.A....?
I'M SORRY, IZUKU.

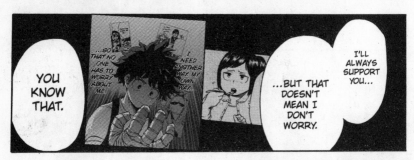

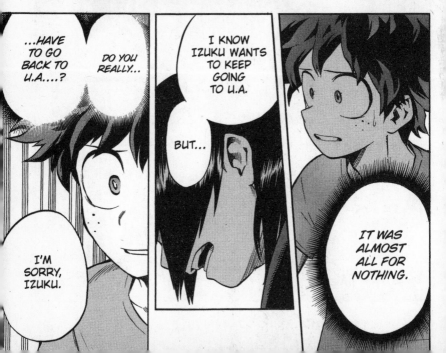

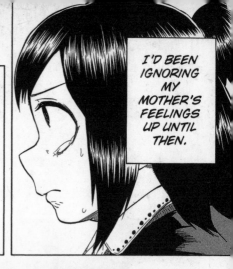

I'D BEEN IGNORING MY MOTHER'S FEELINGS UP UNTIL THEN.
THIS WAS THE OBVIOUS CONSEQUENCE ...
LET ME SPEAK PLAINLY.
WHOOSH
AS IZUKU'S MOTHER...

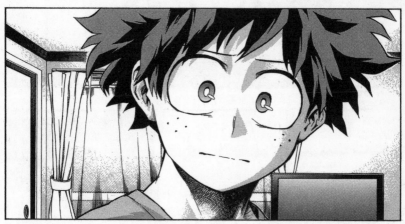

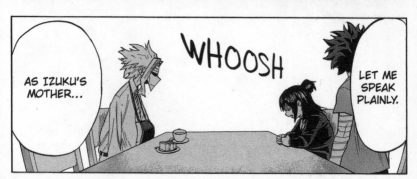

WITH U.A. IN THE STATE IT'S IN...
RRM
BBB
...I CANNOT IN GOOD CONSCIENCE ENTRUST MY SON TO YOUR SCHOOL.
BB
RRMB

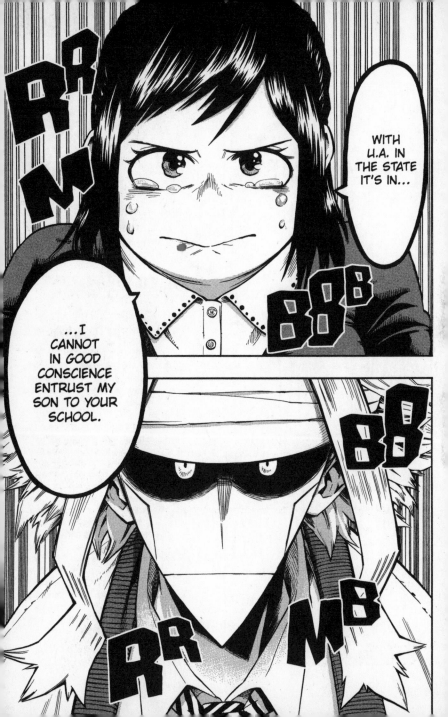

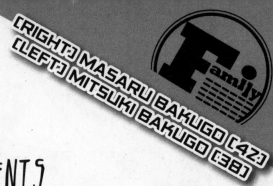

**[RIGHT:] MASARU BAKUGO [42]**
**[LEFT:] MITSUKI BAKUGO [38]**

# PARENTS

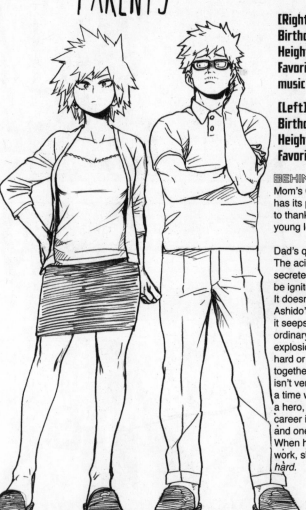

**[Right]**
Birthday: 3/15
Height: 177 cm
Favorite Thing: Classical music

**[Left]**
Birthday: 12/1
Height: 170 cm
Favorite Thing: Volleyball

**BEHIND THE SCENES**
Mom's Quirk is Glycerin. She has its preservative qualities to thank for her good skin. So young looking.

Dad's quirk is Acid Sweat. The acid-like sweat he secretes from his palms can be ignited and detonated. It doesn't gush out the way Ashido's acid does, though—it seeps out little by little, like ordinary sweat. He can cause explosions by clapping really hard or rubbing his hands together. That said, the effect isn't very powerful. There was a time when he wanted to be a hero, but then he found a career in the design industry, and one thing led to another. When he met Mitsuki through work, she came onto him *hard*.

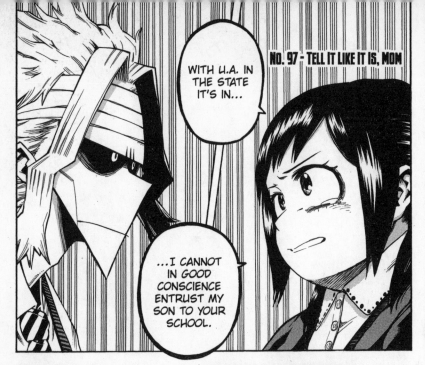

WITH U.A. IN THE STATE IT'S IN...

...I CANNOT IN GOOD CONSCIENCE ENTRUST MY SON TO YOUR SCHOOL.

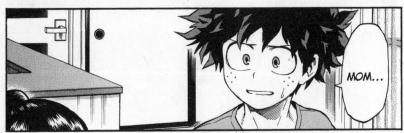

MOM...

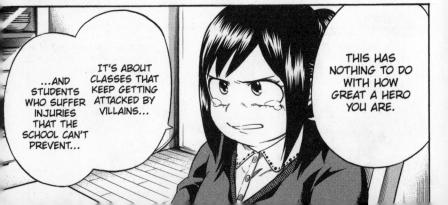

THIS HAS NOTHING TO DO WITH HOW GREAT A HERO YOU ARE.

IT'S ABOUT CLASSES THAT KEEP GETTING ATTACKED BY VILLAINS...

...AND STUDENTS WHO SUFFER INJURIES THAT THE SCHOOL CAN'T PREVENT...

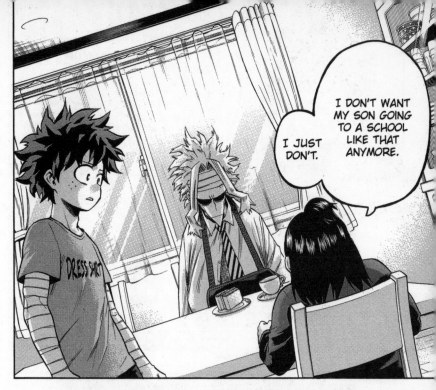

I DON'T WANT MY SON GOING TO A SCHOOL LIKE THAT ANYMORE.

I JUST DON'T.

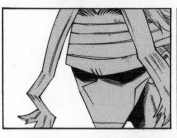

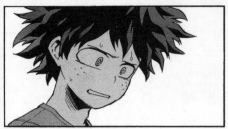

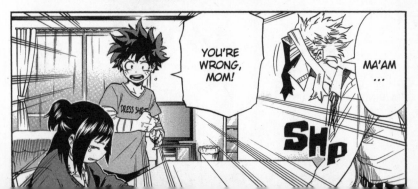

YOU'RE WRONG, MOM!

MA'AM...

SHP

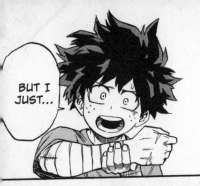

ME GETTING HURT WAS MY OWN FAULT!
THE TEACHERS GAVE ME WARNING AFTER WARNING...
BUT I JUST...
IF THIS IS HOW IT TURNS OUT, THOUGH...
IT'S STILL THE SCHOOL'S RESPONSIBILITY.
KID.
TAKE A SEAT.
YOU CAN CALL ME A HELICOPTER PARENT IF YOU WANT.
I'M FINE WITH THAT.
IT'S NOT THAT I WANT TO RUIN IZUKU'S DREAMS.
IF HE'S STILL INTENT ON BECOMING A HERO...
...THEN THERE ARE PLENTY OF HERO COURSES AT SCHOOLS *OTHER* THAN U.A.

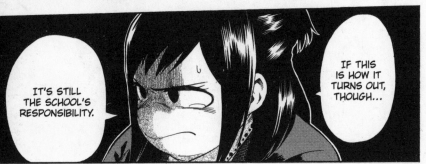

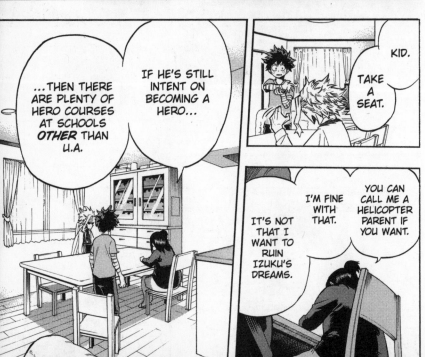

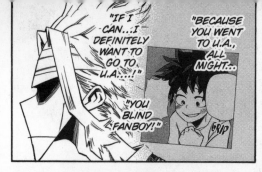

"BECAUSE YOU WENT TO U.A., ALL MIGHT..."
"IF I CAN...I DEFINITELY WANT TO GO TO U.A....!"
"YOU BLIND FANBOY!"
GRIP
LESS SHIRT
FROM NOW ON, I CAN FOCUS ON RAISING YOU RIGHT.
MUST BE HARD FOR HIM TO TAKE...

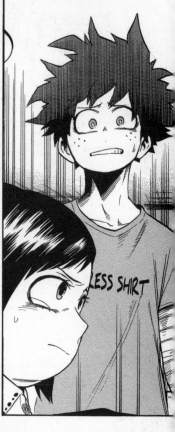

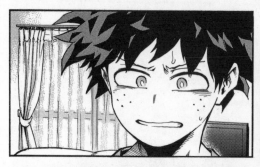

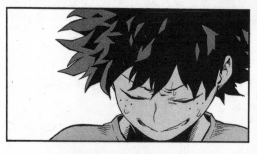

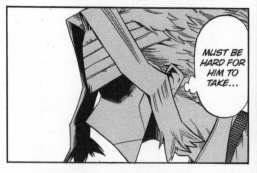

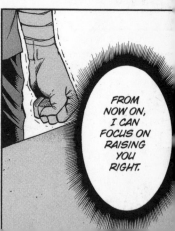

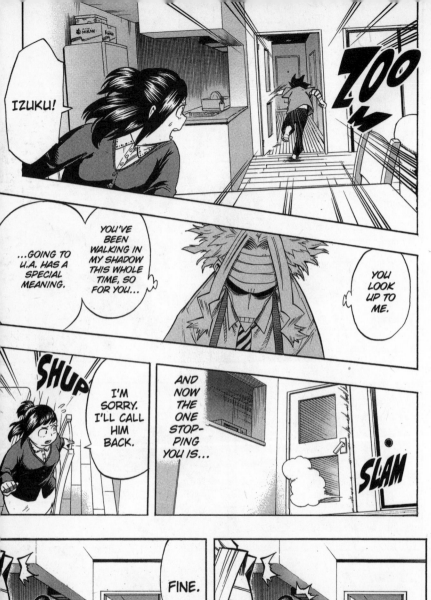

ZOOM
IZUKU!
YOU LOOK UP TO ME.
YOU'VE BEEN WALKING IN MY SHADOW THIS WHOLE TIME, SO FOR YOU...
...GOING TO U.A. HAS A SPECIAL MEANING.
AND NOW THE ONE STOP-PING YOU IS...
SLAM
I'M SORRY. I'LL CALL HIM BACK.
SHUP
FINE.

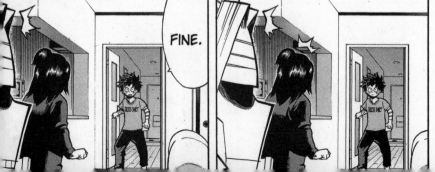

IT DOESN'T HAVE TO BE U.A.
LOOK.
MOM. ALL MIGHT.
LOOK AT THIS LETTER I GOT.
To Midoriya,
Sorry I punched you in the junk.
Thanks for saving me when you didn't even know me.
Get better soon so I can thank you in person.
-Kota
DRESS SH
IT'S FROM A KID I RESCUED DURING OUR TRAINING CAMP.
HE HATED HEROES AND QUIRKS, BUT STILL...
HE WROTE TO ME JUST TO SAY THANK YOU.

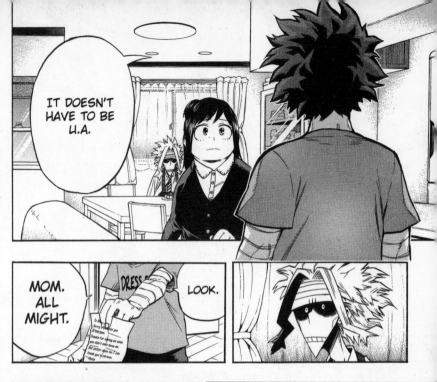

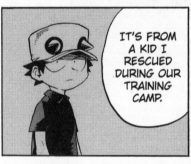

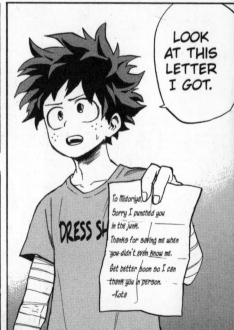

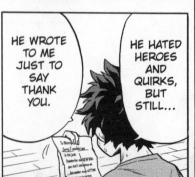

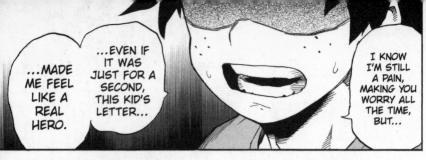

I KNOW I'M STILL A PAIN, MAKING YOU WORRY ALL THE TIME, BUT...
...EVEN IF IT WAS JUST FOR A SECOND, THIS KID'S LETTER...
...MADE ME FEEL LIKE A REAL HERO.
I WAS SO HAPPY!
AH...
I SEE...
IT DOESN'T HAVE TO BE U.A.... I'LL GO WHEREVER!
YOU'RE...
...FINALLY...
BECAUSE I'M GONNA BE A HERO!

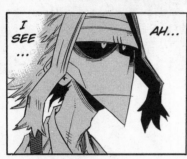

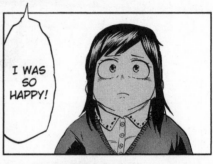

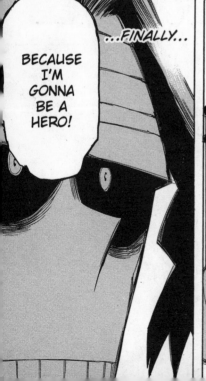

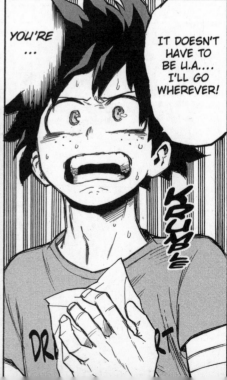

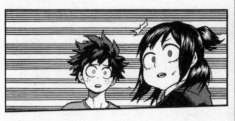

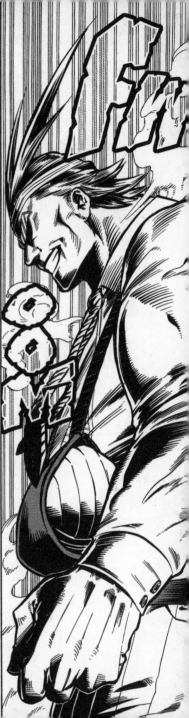

YOU'RE NO LONGER...
...MERELY WALKING IN MY SHADOW!
LOOM
SO AS YOUR TEACHER, I SHOULD SUPPORT YOU!
SORRY FOR GETTING AHEAD OF MYSELF...
SHF

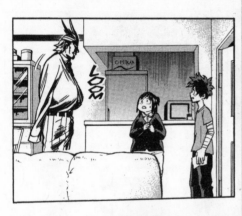

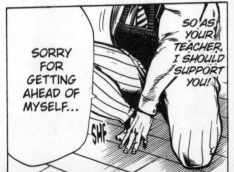

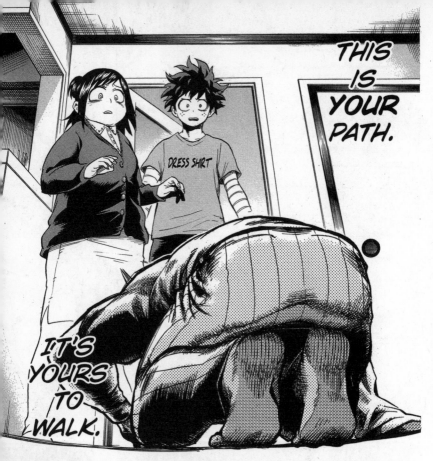

THIS IS YOUR PATH.

DRESS SHIRT

IT'S YOURS TO WALK.

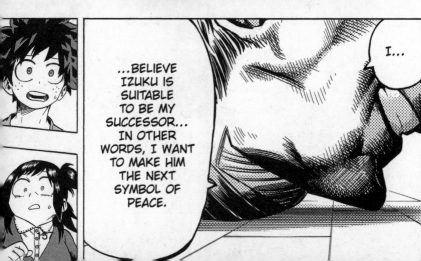

...BELIEVE IZUKU IS SUITABLE TO BE MY SUCCESSOR... IN OTHER WORDS, I WANT TO MAKE HIM THE NEXT SYMBOL OF PEACE.

I...

UH... WHAT? HOLD ON...!! WHAT ARE YOU DOING?
WHAT ?!
AS THE FORMER SYMBOL OF PEACE...I HAVE TO APOLOGIZE.
DRESS SHIRT
I TOOK HIS ADMIRATION FOR GRANTED...
...AND WAS LAX IN HIS EDUCATION. FOR THAT, I'M SORRY!
FSSHH
POOF
SO NOW, AS A TEACHER AT U.A....
...I BEG YOU.

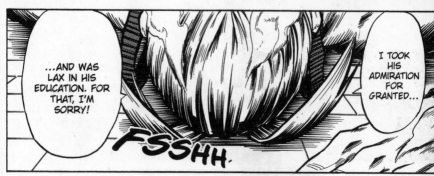

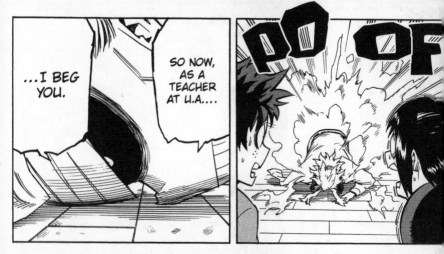

INDEED, THE PATH I WALKED WAS A BLOODY ONE...
BUT THAT'S EXACTLY WHAT I DON'T WANT FOR YOUR SON.
I WILL STAND BY HIM AND HELP HIM FIND HIS OWN PATH.
ALL MIGHT...!
A SUPER-COOL HERO LIKE THAT
IT'S COMPLETELY REASONABLE TO HAVE DOUBTS ABOUT U.A. BECAUSE OF THE STATE IT'S IN.
BUT THE HEROES OF U.A. KNOW THAT...THEY KNOW THAT THINGS HAVE GOT TO CHANGE!
PLEASE DO NOT FOCUS ON THE CURRENT U.A., BUT ON THE U.A. GOING FORWARD...!!
PLEASE ALLOW ME TO...
...DEVOTE MYSELF TO MENTORING IZUKU.

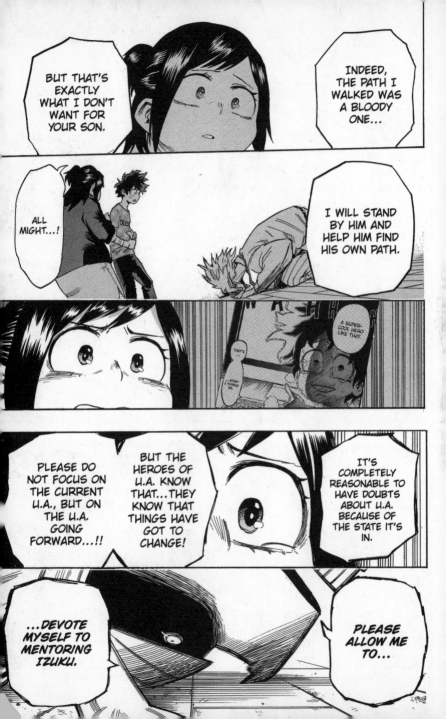

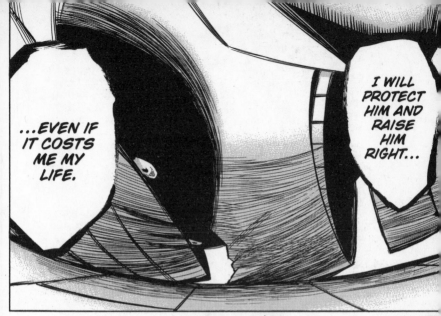

I WILL PROTECT HIM AND RAISE HIM RIGHT...
...EVEN IF IT COSTS ME MY LIFE.
WHUMP
I CAN'T...
...AGREE TO THAT...

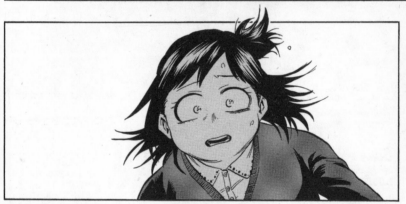

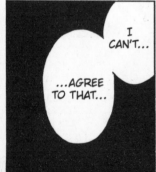

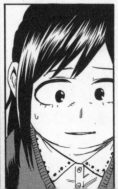

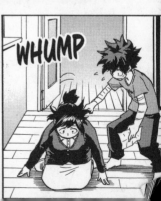

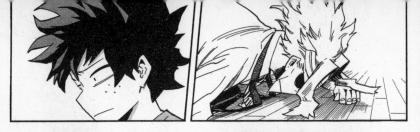

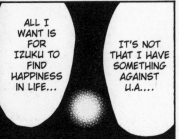

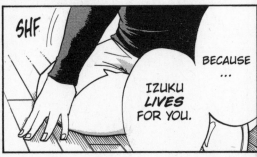

SHF
BECAUSE...
IZUKU *LIVES* FOR YOU.
IT'S NOT THAT I HAVE SOMETHING AGAINST U.A....
ALL I WANT IS FOR IZUKU TO FIND HAPPINESS IN LIFE...
SO DON'T SACRIFICE YOUR LIFE.
LIVE.
AND PLEASE LOOK AFTER HIM.

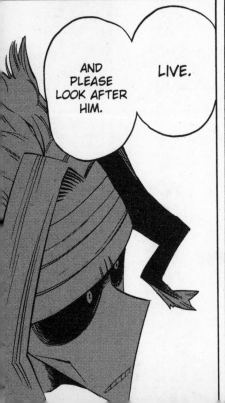

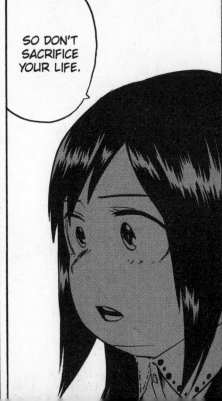

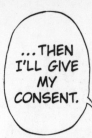

IF YOU CAN PROMISE ME THAT...
...THEN I'LL GIVE MY CONSENT.
MOM ...
YOU HAVE ...
...MY WORD!

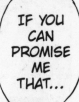

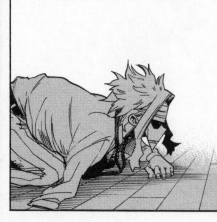

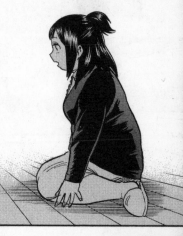

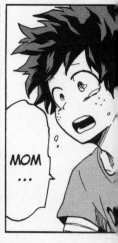

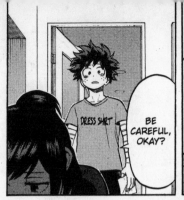

AND, IZUKU...
IF YOU'RE GOING TO LIVE AT U.A. NOW...
DRESS SHIRT
BE CAREFUL, OKAY?
I PROMISE.
YOU WON'T REGRET THIS!
...
DON'T LOOK AT ME LIKE THAT...
HONESTLY...
I DON'T LIKE THIS.
BUT OUR IZUKU, HE...
WITHOUT ME EVEN KNOWING...
HE SOME-HOW MANAGED...
...TO GET ALL THIS SUPPORT FROM THE HERO HE LOOKS UP TO.
I'M SURE...
...THIS IS MAKING YOU TRULY HAPPY.

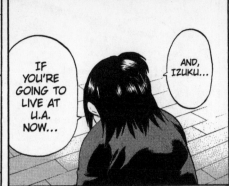

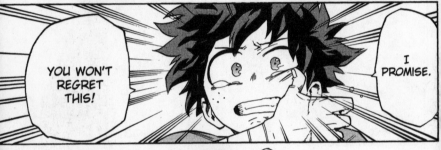

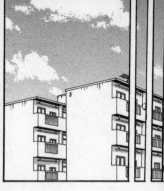

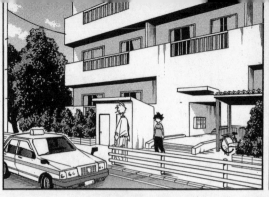

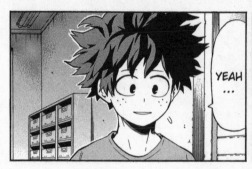

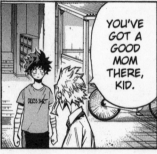

YOU'VE GOT A GOOD MOM THERE, KID.
YEAH ...
LIVE.
LIVING THE LIFE OF A NATURAL-BORN HERO... IT'S BEEN A WHILE SINCE I'VE HEARD THAT.
SHE REMINDS ME OF MY MASTER. MY PREDECESSOR ...
HUH?! MY MOM DOES...?!
YEAH. HER HAIRSTYLE.
HER HAIR...

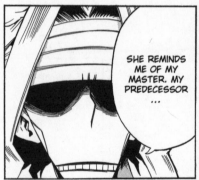

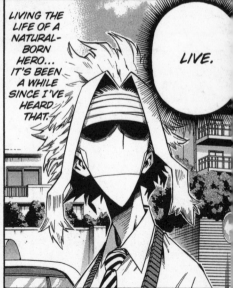

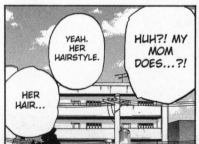

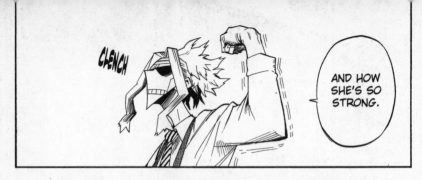

CLENCH
AND HOW SHE'S SO STRONG.
HUH?! LOOK AT THAT WEIRD SKELETON MAN. COULD THAT BE...?!
CRAP. GUESS *THIS* FORM IS NOW ALL MIGHT TOO! I'M NOT USED TO THAT.
SEE YOU AT SCHOOL, THEN!!
Okay!
FIDGET
FIDGET
VOOSH

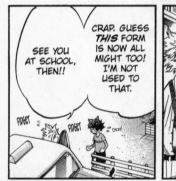

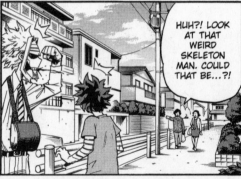

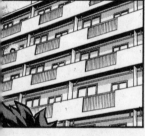

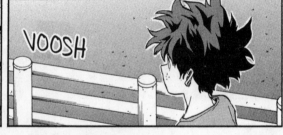

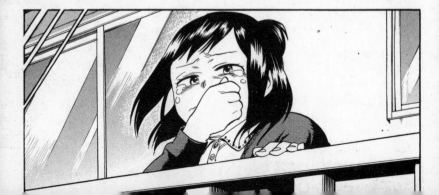

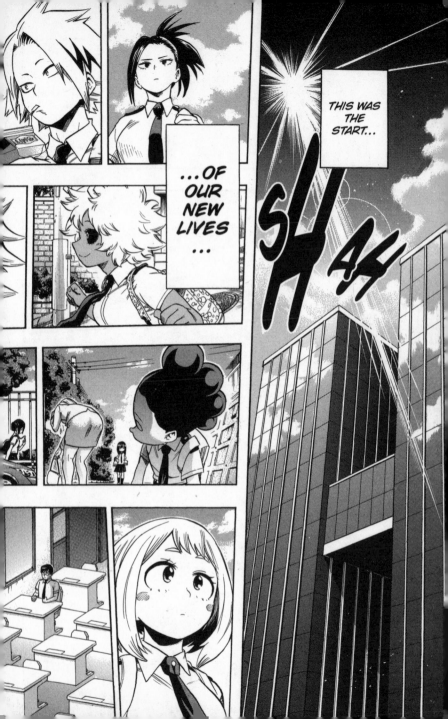

THIS WAS THE START...

...OF OUR NEW LIVES...

SHAA

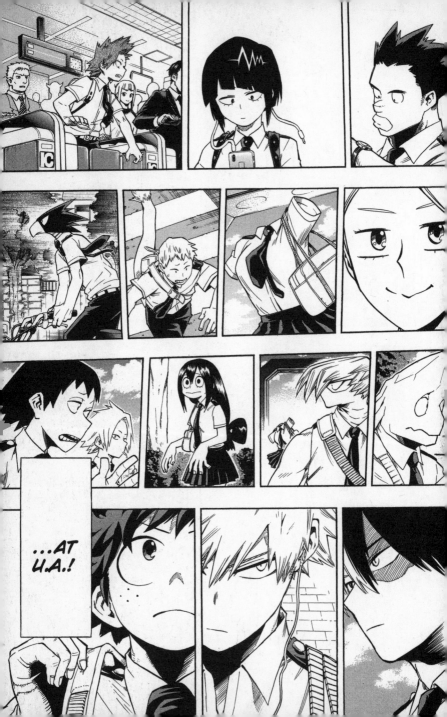

...AT
U.A.!

Family

**[RIGHT] KYOTOKU JIRO [40]**
**[LEFT] MIKA JIRO [36]**

# PARENTS



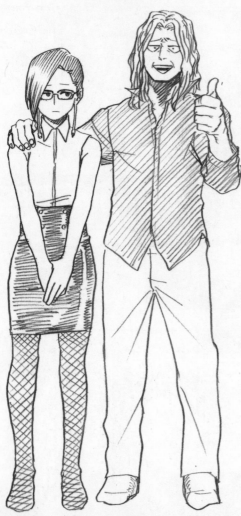

**[Right]**
**Birthday: 1/16**
**Height: 171 cm**
**Favorite Thing: Rock music**

**[Left]**
**Birthday: 2/16**
**Height: 159 cm**
**Favorite Thing: Punk music**

## BEHIND THE SCENES

The earphone jacks are mom's Quirk, which she passed down to Jiro along with her disposition. It's pretty common for children to inherit the mother's personality when the parents have very different ones.

Dad is a composer who was charmed by his wife-to-be's musical talent.

As both parents have lived their lives doing what they love to do, they also encourage their daughter to walk her own path. Do your best, Daughter!

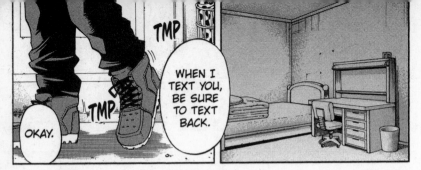

TMP
WHEN I TEXT YOU, BE SURE TO TEXT BACK.
TMP
OKAY.
BE SURE TO EAT RIGHT, OKAY?
YUP.
No. 98 - Moving into Dorms
MID-AUGUST... TODAY IS THE DAY...
I STILL...
...DON'T LIKE THIS.
...I LEAVE HOME.
MM...

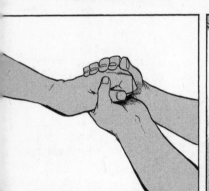

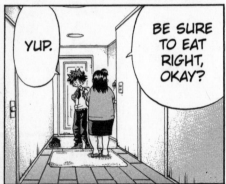

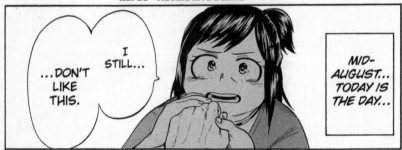

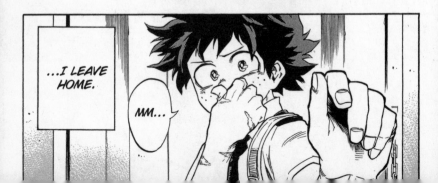

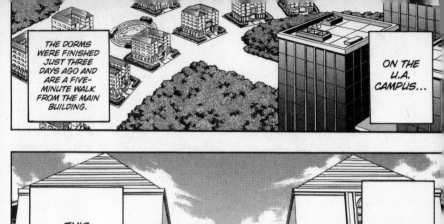

ON THE U.A. CAMPUS...
THE DORMS WERE FINISHED JUST THREE DAYS AGO AND ARE A FIVE-MINUTE WALK FROM THE MAIN BUILDING.
HEIGHTS ALLIANCE ...
THIS IS MY NEW... NO...
1-A
ALLIANCE
No. 98 - Moving Into Dorms
OUR NEW HOME!
IT'S HUGE!
WE'RE SOME LUCKY KIDS!

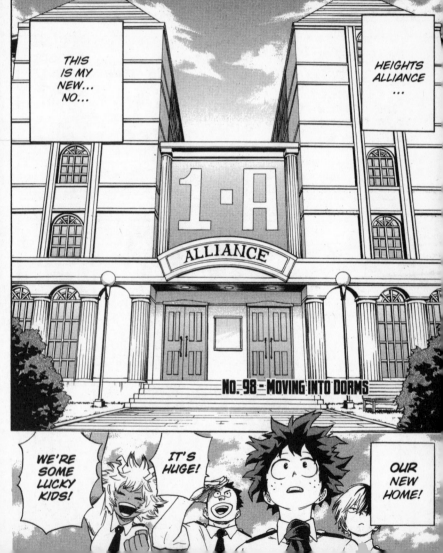

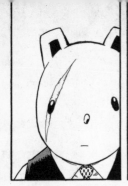

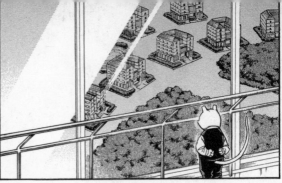

THESE DORMS AREN'T JUST TO ENSURE THE STUDENTS' SAFETY.
WE'LL ALSO BE ABLE TO DEAL WITH ANY THREATS WE HAVEN'T TAKEN CARE OF YET... IN OTHER WORDS, A POTENTIAL MOLE.
IN ORDER TO PUT AN END TO THE SUSPICIONS THAT HAVE BEEN ARISING FOR A WHILE NOW...
...IT'S BEST TO AVOID A PUBLIC INVESTIGATION. WE'LL SEARCH FOR THE PERPETRATOR IN SECRET.
THOUGH IT PAINS ME TO SUSPECT NOT ONLY TEACHERS BUT ALSO THE STUDENTS...
...GIVEN MY POSITION, IT'S WHAT MUST BE DONE.
WE'RE STARTING TO FEEL THE EFFECTS OF LOSING OUR "SYMBOL" MORE AND MORE AS TIME PASSES...
WHAT WE NEED NOW IS A REVIVAL.
AT LEAST FOR THE STUDENTS...
WE NEED TO PRESENT THEM WITH PROSPECTS OF A BRIGHT FUTURE...

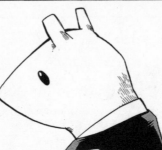

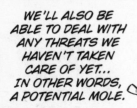

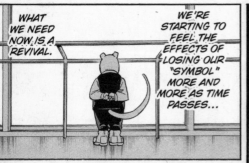

NOW THEN, CLASS 1-A...
SHAH
I'M GLAD TO SEE YOU ALL HERE.
LOOKS LIKE EVERYONE GOT PERMISSION TO MOVE IN...
SIGH
IT WAS AN UPHILL BATTLE FOR ME...
MAKES SENSE...
RIGHT. PROBABLY CUZ YOU TWO WERE INJURED BY THAT GAS AND HOSPITALIZED.
AND WE'RE GLAD TO SEE YOU HERE, SENSEI.
I WAS SAD CUZ I THOUGHT YOU MIGHT NOT COME BACK AFTER THAT PRESS CONFERENCE.
MM...
I'M SURPRISED TOO.
BUT, WELL... A LOT'S HAPPENED.
I SUSPECT... RATHER THAN SHAKING THINGS UP FOR THE WORSE, THEY LET ME OFF THE HOOK, KNOWING THEY'D ALWAYS HAVE THAT OVER ME.
OR SOME-THING LIKE THAT...
ANY-WAY...
I'M GONNA GIVE A QUICK OVERVIEW OF YOUR DORMS.
BUT BEFORE THAT...
CLAP

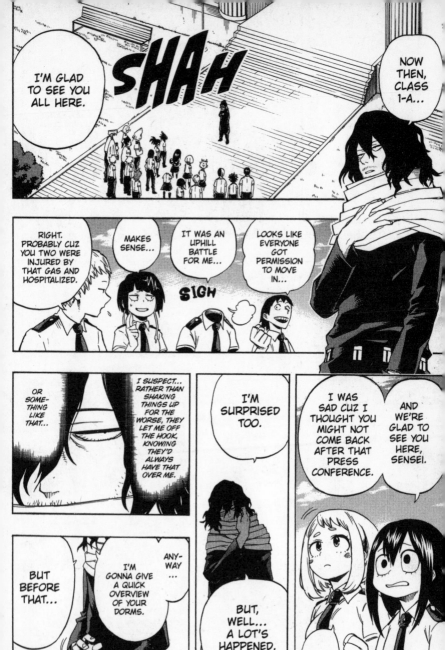

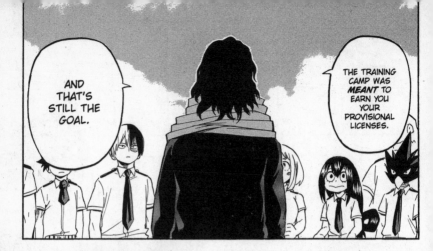

THE TRAINING CAMP WAS *MEANT* TO EARN YOU YOUR PROVISIONAL LICENSES.
AND THAT'S STILL THE GOAL.
OH YEAH, THAT'S RIGHT! THAT'S WHAT WE WERE DOING.
WITH EVERYTHING THAT HAPPENED, I TOTALLY FORGOT...
THIS IS IMPORTANT. LISTEN UP.
TODOROKI.
KIRISHIMA.
MIDORIYA.
YAOYO-ROZU.
IDA.
ON *THAT* NIGHT, YOU FIVE HEADED OUT...
...TO RESCUE BAKUGO.

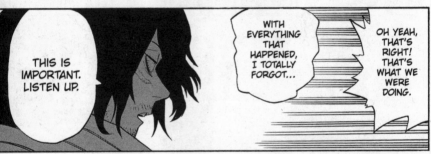

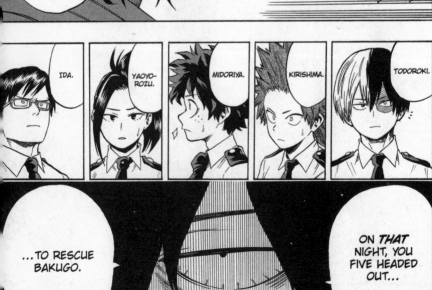

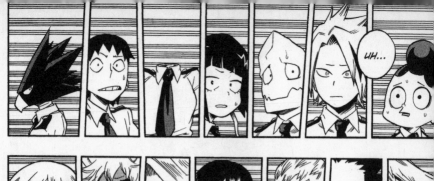

UH...
I THINK THAT ALL OF YOU HERE...
...UNDER-STAND THE CONSEQUENCES OF THOSE ACTIONS.
THE ISSUE'S BEEN SWEPT UNDER THE RUG FOR NOW, BUT LET ME SAY THIS MUCH.
IF NOT FOR ALL MIGHT'S RETIREMENT...
I WOULD HAVE EXPELLED EVERY SINGLE ONE OF YOU, EXCEPT FOR BAKUGO, JIRO AND HAGAKURE.
WHOOSH
?!

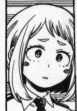

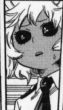

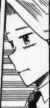

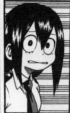

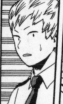

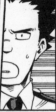

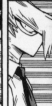

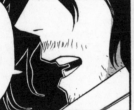

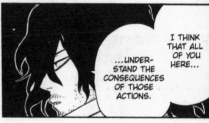

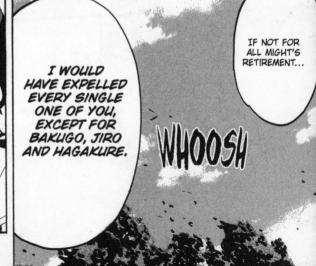

THE CHAOS IS SURE TO CONTINUE NOW THAT HE'S RETIRED... AND SINCE WE CAN'T GET A READ ON THE LEAGUE OF VILLAINS' NEXT MOVE, KICKING ANYONE OUT OF U.A. AT PRESENT IS ILL-ADVISED.
THE FIVE WHO WENT, OF COURSE...
BUT ALSO THE 12 WHO KNEW BUT DID NOTHING TO STOP THEM...
YOUR REASONS ASIDE...
THE FACT REMAINS THAT YOU BETRAYED OUR TRUST.
FROM THIS POINT ON, IF YOU FOLLOW PROCEDURES AND BEHAVE PROPERLY...
...YOU MIGHT BE ABLE TO REGAIN OUR TRUST.
FWIP
THAT'S ALL! NOW LOOK LIVELY AND GET A MOVE ON!
TMP
TMP
LIVELY? AFTER THAT...?!

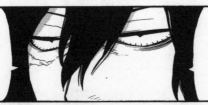

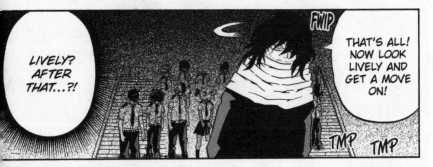

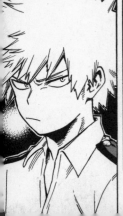

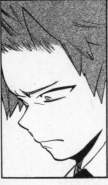

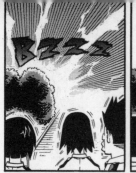

COME.
YANK
HUH? WHAT? STOP IT!
BZZZ
YAYYY...
BURST!
!!
PFFT...
PFFT...
HUH? WHAT'D YOU DO, BAKUGO...?
WORMP WORMP
KIRI-SHIMA.
WHA-?
EH. TOO SCARY, DUDE. YOU SHOOK HIM DOWN FOR THAT?!
FWIP
WRONG. I BROUGHT THIS CASH MYSELF!

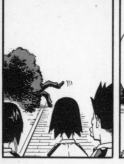

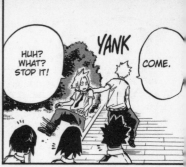

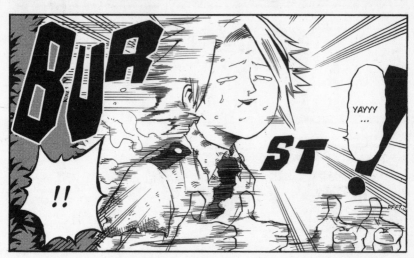

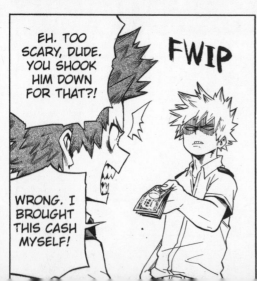

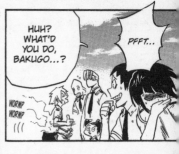

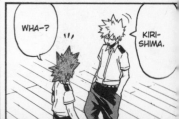

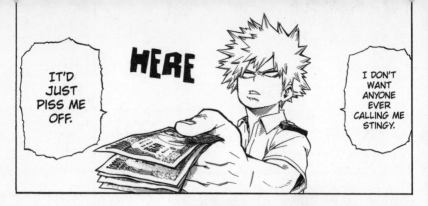

I DON'T WANT ANYONE EVER CALLING ME STINGY.
HERE
IT'D JUST PISS ME OFF.
NIGHT VISION BINOCULARS
49,800 YEN ONLINE
AH... HUH?! HOW'D YOU KNOW?
YAYY ...?
YAYYY YAYY YAYY YAYYY ?!
WORD ALWAYS GETS OUT WITH SO MANY IDIOTS AROUND.
OH MAN... THAT'S OUR KAMINARI FOR YA.
PFFFT !!
FAYY... FAYY, FADEAWAYYY ...
SHUP
Bwa ha ha ha...
...
THANKS, MAN.
Hahhh! Hee hee...
You're laughing too hard.
Ha ha ha ha...
GOOFING AROUND, HUH...?
SOMETIMES THAT'S EXACTLY WHAT YOU NEED...

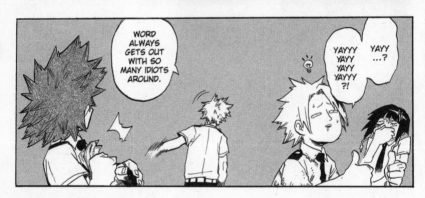

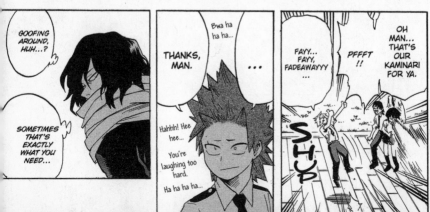

YOU GUYS! I'M SORRY...!! I KNOW I CAN'T REALLY MAKE IT UP TO YOU, BUT...
THIS MONEY'S GONNA GO INTO SOME BARBECUE FOR EVERYONE TONIGHT!!
YEAHHH!
YEAHHH!
YAYYY!
THINK WE COULD ALSO DO SOME SHOPPING?
Ura-raka
WHOA, FOR REAL?
Sero
HAHHH! HEE HEE...
Jiro
ONE CLASS TO EACH BUILDING. GIRLS ON THE RIGHT, BOYS ON THE LEFT.
THE FIRST FLOOR IS A COMMON AREA.
YOUR DINING HALL, BATHS AND LAUNDRY ROOMS ARE HERE.
SO SPACIOUS!! WOWWW!!!
Ooh!
WE'VE EVEN GOT A COURTYARD!
SWANKY LIVIN'.
WOBBLE
Uraraka !!

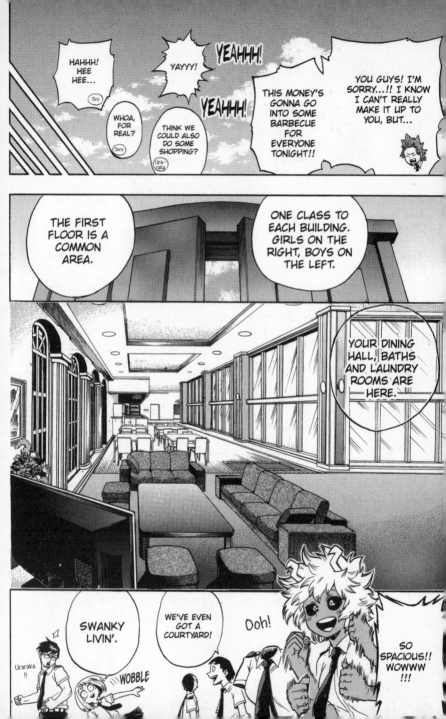

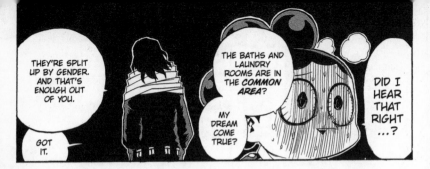

DID I HEAR THAT RIGHT ...?
THE BATHS AND LAUNDRY ROOMS ARE IN THE *COMMON AREA*?
MY DREAM COME TRUE?
THEY'RE SPLIT UP BY GENDER. AND THAT'S ENOUGH OUT OF YOU.
GOT IT.
DING...
B1 1 2 3 4 5
THE ROOMS START ON THE SECOND FLOOR.
FOUR BOYS' ROOMS AND FOUR GIRLS' ROOMS ON EACH FLOOR, FIVE FLOORS IN ALL.
ONE STUDENT PER ROOM.
YOU'VE GOT AIR CONDITIONERS, TOILETS, REFRIGERATORS AND CLOSETS.
ENJOY THE LUXURIES.
WE EVEN HAVE VERANDAS!
WOW!
THE CLOSETS HERE ARE JUST AS BIG AS MINE BACK HOME...
SWANKY LIVIN'...
Wahhh...

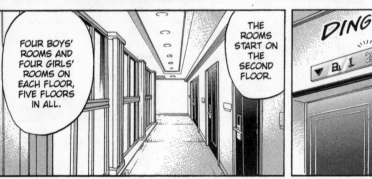

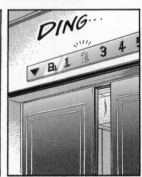

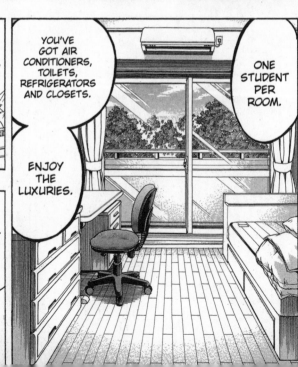

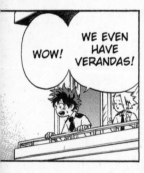

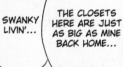

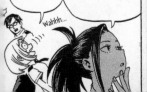

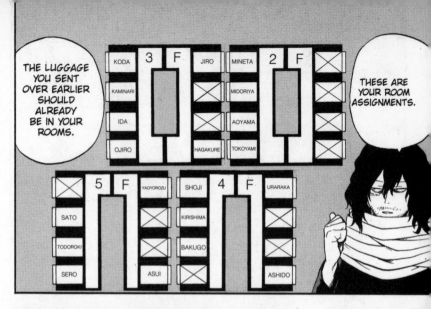

THESE ARE YOUR ROOM ASSIGNMENTS.
THE LUGGAGE YOU SENT OVER EARLIER SHOULD ALREADY BE IN YOUR ROOMS.
2 F
MINETA
MIDORIYA
AOYAMA
TOKOYAMI
3 F
JIRO
HAGAKURE
KODA
KAMINARI
IDA
OJIRO
4 F
URARAKA
ASHIDO
SHOJI
KIRISHIMA
BAKUGO
5 F
YAOYOROZU
ASUI
SATO
TODOROKI
SERO
TODAY'S SET ASIDE FOR SETTLING IN. WE'LL TALK ABOUT WHAT COMES NEXT TOMORROW.
DISMISSED!
YES, SENSEI!!
Raglan T-Shirt

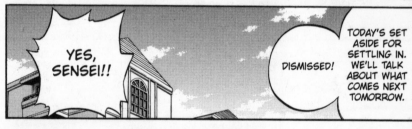

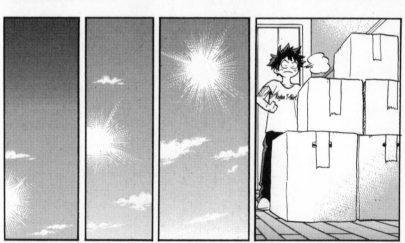

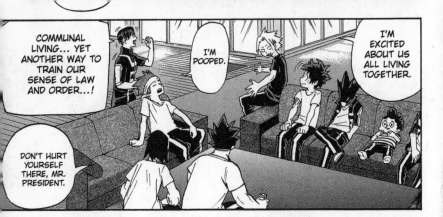

I'M EXCITED ABOUT US ALL LIVING TOGETHER.
I'M POOPED.
COMMUNAL LIVING... YET ANOTHER WAY TO TRAIN OUR SENSE OF LAW AND ORDER...!
DON'T HURT YOURSELF THERE, MR. PRESIDENT.
YOU BOYS ALL FINISHED WITH YOUR ROOMS?
GIRLS
GIRLS
Oh, it's the girls!
YEAH, WE'RE JUST RELAXING NOW.
SO YEAH! WE'VE BEEN TALKING, AND WE'VE GOT AN IDEA!
HOW ABOUT WE HAVE...
...A PEEK INTO EACH OTHER'S ROOMS?!

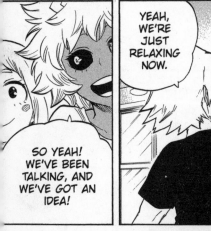

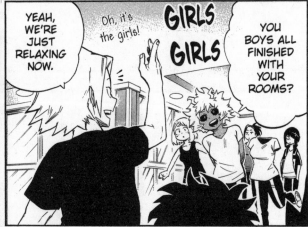

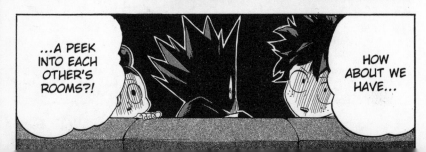

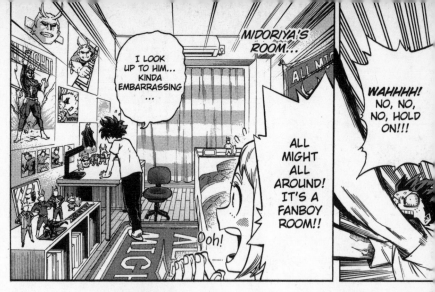

WAHHHH! NO, NO, NO, HOLD ON!!!
MIDORIYA'S ROOM...
ALL MIGHT ALL AROUND! IT'S A FANBOY ROOM!!
I LOOK UP TO HIM... KINDA EMBARRASSING...
Ooh!
UH-OH. WHAT HAVE WE GOTTEN OURSELVES INTO HERE...?
GULP
COULD BE FUN, THOUGH...
HMPH!
RIDICULOUS...
SHOVE

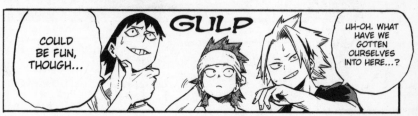

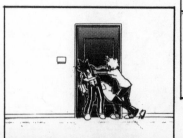

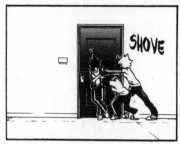

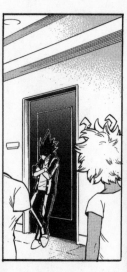

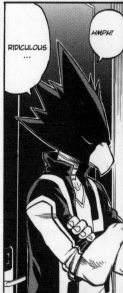

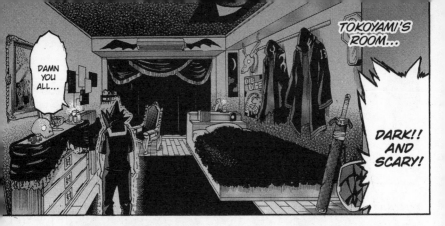

TOKOYAMI'S ROOM...
DARK!! AND SCARY!
DAMN YOU ALL...
I REMEMBER BUYING KEY CHAINS LIKE THIS IN MIDDLE SCHOOL.
SO BOYS LIKE THINGS LIKE THIS, HUH?
Real swords...
SO COOL.
BE-GONE!!
AOYAMA'S ROOM...
SHINY!!
HA HA HA HA HA HA
NON, NON... NOT SHINY.
TWINKLY!
PRETTY MUCH WHAT WE EXPECTED.
NOTHING SURPRISING, REALLY.

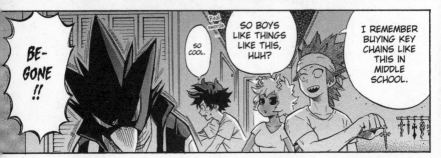

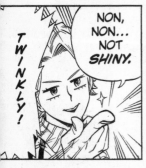

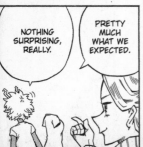

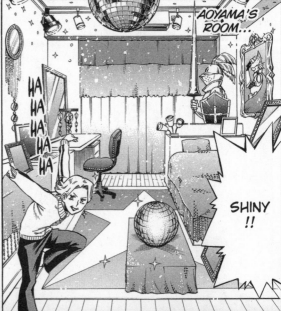

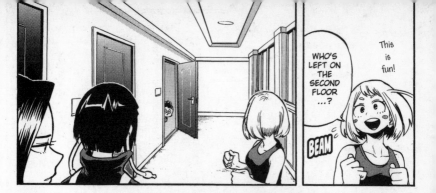

This is fun!
WHO'S LEFT ON THE SECOND FLOOR...?
BEAM
COME ON IN...
HAHH
HAHH
HAHH
I'VE GOT... SOMETHING AWESOME TO SHOW YOU.
TIME FOR THE THIRD FLOOR.
HAHH
COME ON IN...?
HAHH
OJIRO'S ROOM...
WHOA!! IT REALLY IS PLAIN!
YUP. JUST ABOUT THE PLAINEST ROOM YOU COULD HAVE...!
WOW, SO PLAIN!!
IF YOU'VE GOT NOTHING NICE TO SAY...

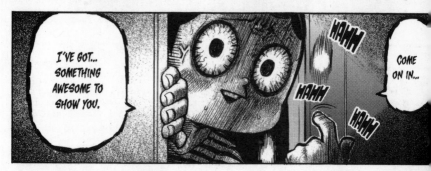

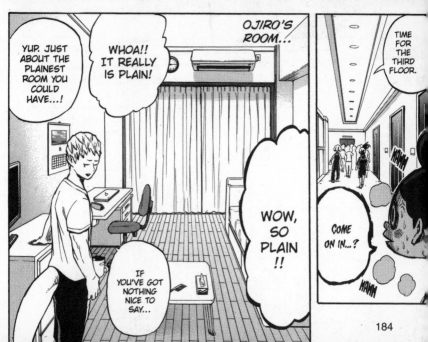

IDA'S ROOM...
NOTHING OUT OF THE ORDINARY HERE.
ALL THESE HIGH-LEVEL BOOKS... THAT'S OUR CLASS PRESIDENT FOR YOU!
HE'S OBSESSED WITH GLASSES!
PFFT!
IS THAT SO UNREASONABLE?! I EXPECT TO GO THROUGH MANY PAIRS DURING OUR INTENSE TRAINING...
KAMINARI'S ROOM...
IT'S JUST FUN AND GAMES!
YOU DON'T LIKE IT?!
HE'S GOT A LITTLE OF EVERYTHING!
KODA'S ROOM...
THERE'S A BUNNY!! TOO CUTE!!
NO FAIR, USING A PET LIKE THAT. THAT'S CHEATING, KODA.
LOOKS LIKE WE'RE STARTING TO GET COMPETITIVE...
Cute!
Cute!

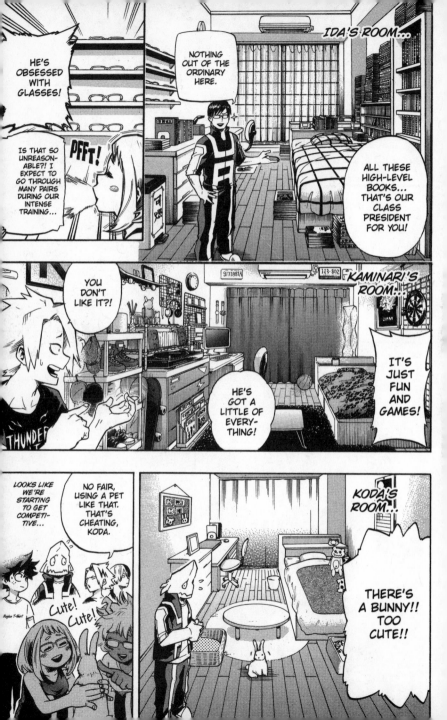

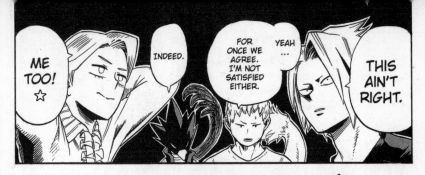

THIS AIN'T RIGHT.
YEAH ...
FOR ONCE WE AGREE. I'M NOT SATISFIED EITHER.
INDEED.
ME TOO! ☆
ISN'T IT WEIRD THAT ONLY THE BOYS HAD TO PRESENT THEIR ROOMS?
WHOOOSH
THIS IS AN *EXHIBITION*, RIGHT?
SO IF WE'RE GONNA PICK A WINNER, THEN IT'S ONLY NATURAL THAT WE SEE THE GIRLS' ROOMS TOO!
WHO'S THE BEST INTERIOR DECORATOR IN THE CLASS?
THAT'S WHAT WE'RE HERE TO DECIDE!!

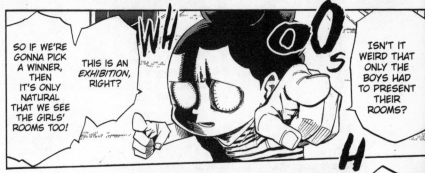

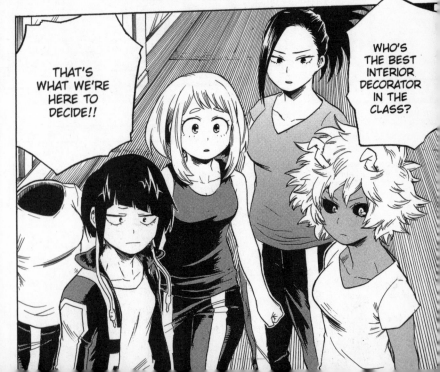

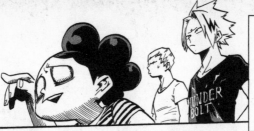

THE GIRLS' NO-HOLDS-BARRED CRITICISM ...
...STOKED THE COMPETITIVE FIRE IN THE BOYS.
GREAT IDEA.
THE FIRST OFFICIAL CLASS 1-A "BEST AESTHETIC SENSE" CONTEST...
UH...
...WAS ABOUT TO BEGIN!!
IS THIS OKAY...?
GULP
IS THIS REALLY OKAY?!

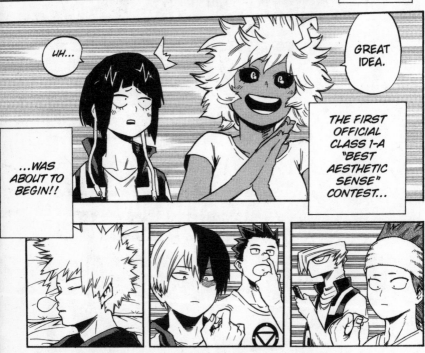

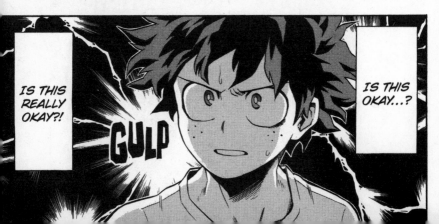

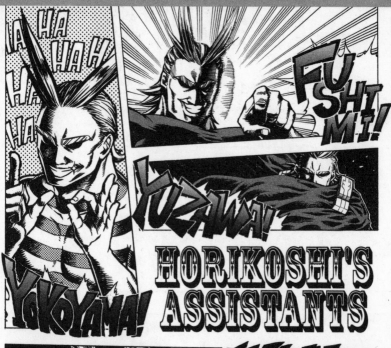

FUSHIMI!
YUZAWA!
HORIKOSHI'S ASSISTANTS
HA HA HA HA HA HA HA HA
YOKOYAMA!
IKEDA!
FUJIYA.
I screwed that up. ♡
Nooo!!
GUCHI!
MONJI!
THEY'RE ALL GREAT PEOPLE. I COULDN'T DO THIS WITHOUT THEM.

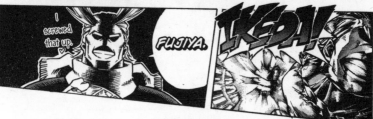

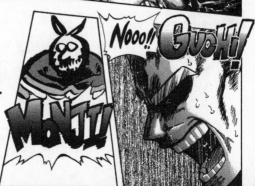

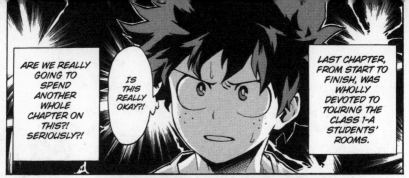

LAST CHAPTER, FROM START TO FINISH, WAS WHOLLY DEVOTED TO TOURING THE CLASS 1-A STUDENTS' ROOMS.
IS THIS REALLY OKAY?!
ARE WE REALLY GOING TO SPEND ANOTHER WHOLE CHAPTER ON THIS?! SERIOUSLY?!
NO. 99 - GOODBYE TWO-DIGIT CHAPTERS, HELLO THREE DIGITS
SO...WE'RE HERE TO DECIDE THE KING OF ROOMS!
KING OF ROOMS?
IT'S FINE IF WE DON'T DO THIS. REALLY...
HEH HEH HEH... IF I WAS THE ONE CALLING FOR THIS, THEY'D SHUT ME DOWN LIKE USUAL.
BUT NOW!
THEIR PRIDE'S ON THE LINE, AND I'M CASHING IN.
YOU CAN'T OPPOSE THE WILL OF THE PEOPLE, AND I GET TO HITCH A FREE RIDE!!
NOW IT'LL TOTALLY HAPPEN NATURALLY.
I GET TO FEAST MY EYES ON THE GIRLS' ROOMS!
I'M TIRED...

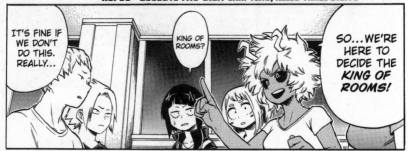

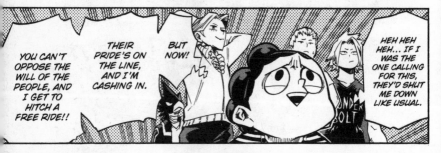

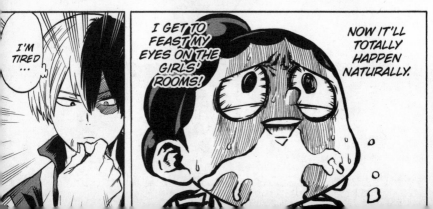

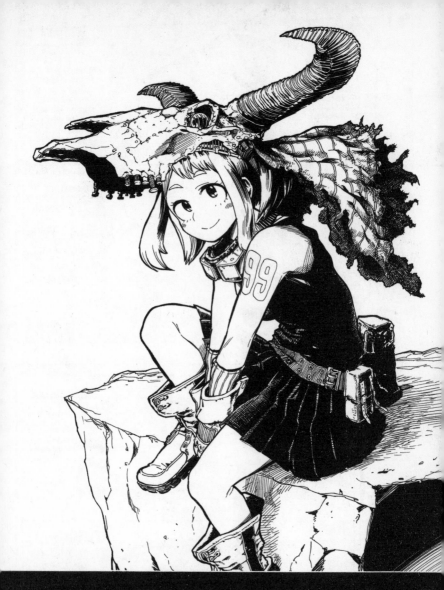

# MY HERO ACADEMIA

## NO. 99 - GOODBYE TWO-DIGIT CHAPTERS, HELLO THREE DIGITS

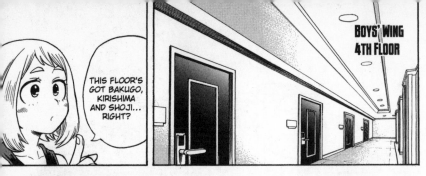

BOYS' WING
4TH FLOOR
THIS FLOOR'S GOT BAKUGO, KIRISHIMA AND SHOJI... RIGHT?
WHERE IS BAKUGO, BY THE WAY?
HE SAID, "THIS IS DUMB. I'M GOING TO BED." I'M GETTING TIRED TOO...
THEN YOUR ROOM'S NEXT, KIRISHIMA!! LET'S PICK UP THE PACE!!
WHATEVER YOU SAY. YOU GIRLS PROBABLY WON'T GET IT, THOUGH...
KIRISHIMA'S ROOM
THIS MANLINESS !!
A.YAZAWA
必勝
BURNING UP WITH MANLINESS !!
HMM...

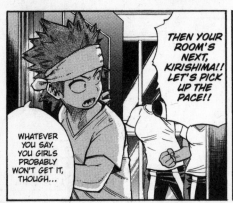

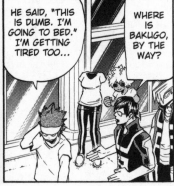

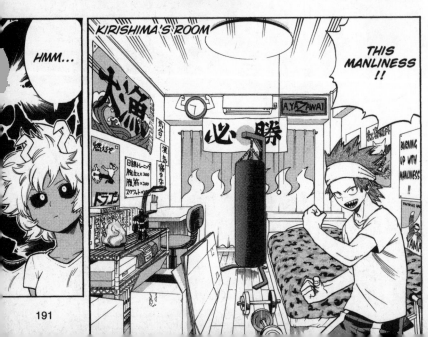

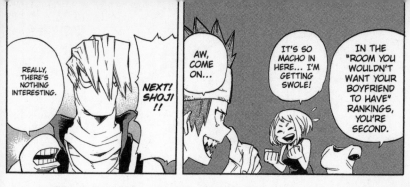

IN THE "ROOM YOU WOULDN'T WANT YOUR BOYFRIEND TO HAVE" RANKINGS, YOU'RE SECOND.
IT'S SO MACHO IN HERE... I'M GETTING SWOLE!
AW, COME ON...
NEXT! SHOJI!!
REALLY, THERE'S NOTHING INTERESTING.
SHOJI'S ROOM
NOTHING INTERESTING? MORE LIKE NOTHING AT ALL!!
GONG
YOU HAVE A REALLY SIMPLE STYLE.
YEAH. EVER SINCE I WAS LITTLE, I'VE NEVER CARED MUCH ABOUT OWNING STUFF.
GUYS LIKE YOU ALWAYS TURN OUT TO BE THE BIGGEST PERVS.
LET'S HEAD UP! FIFTH-FLOOR BOYS ARE NEXT!
WE'LL START WITH SERO!
WE'RE SERIOUSLY GOING TO EVERY ROOM?!
SERO'S ROOM
OOH!!

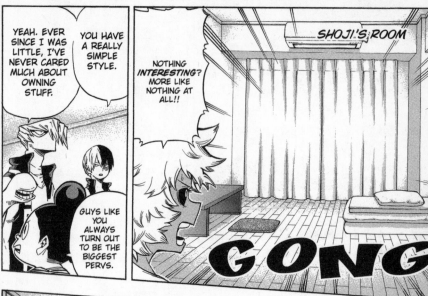

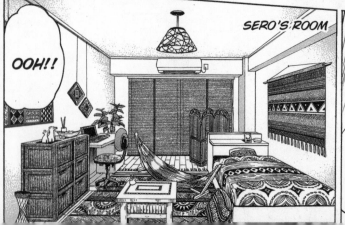

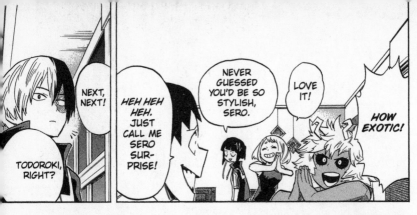

HOW EXOTIC!
LOVE IT!
NEVER GUESSED YOU'D BE SO STYLISH, SERO.
HEH HEH HEH. JUST CALL ME SERO SUR-PRISE!
NEXT, NEXT!
TODOROKI, RIGHT?
OUR CLASS'S MOST CAPABLE STUDENT...
OUR CLASS'S BEST-LOOKING GUY.
WHAT COULD THE ALWAYS-COOL TODOROKI'S ROOM BE LIKE...? I'M ON PINS AND NEEDLES...
LET'S JUST GET THIS OVER WITH...
I'M TIRED.
KLIK
A JAPANESE-STYLE ROOM!!
JAPANESE
IT'S EVEN BUILT DIFFER-ENTLY THAN OURS!

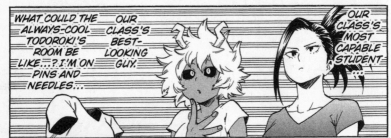

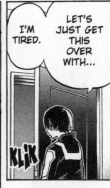

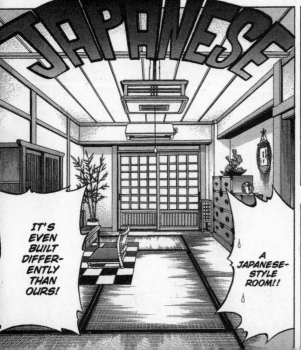

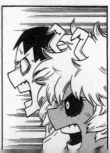

MY FAMILY HOME IS TRADITIONALLY JAPANESE, SO I DON'T LIKE MODERN FLOORING.
WHO CARES WHY?
HOW'DJA REMODEL YOUR ROOM IN ONE DAY?
HARD WORK ...
WHAT'S UP WITH THIS GUY?!
HE SURE IS GOING PLACES.
THE GOOD-LOOKING GUYS ALWAYS HAVE TRICKS UP THEIR SLEEVES.
NEXT!
THE LAST BOY IS...
ME.
SATO'S ROOM
MY ROOM'S KIND OF BORING, REALLY.
sugar
Sweets
EVERY ROOM'S PRETTY MUCH THE SAME AFTER TODOROKI'S.
SOMETHING SURE SMELLS GOOD, THOUGH. WHAT IS IT?
OH NO!! I WAS IN SUCH A RUSH THAT I MUST'VE FORGOTTEN TO FINISH THIS...
Ack!!
I WAS BAKING A CHIFFON CAKE!
I WANTED TO SHARE IT WITH EVERYONE...
THUNDER BOLT

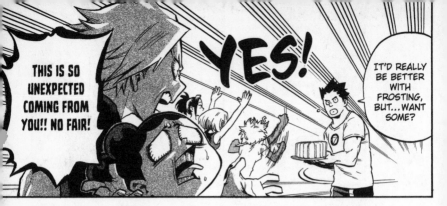

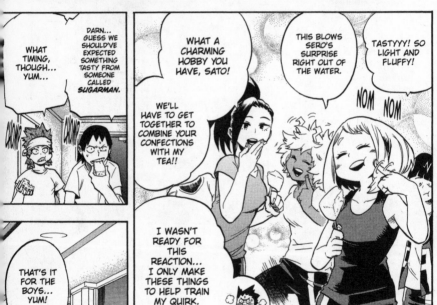

IT'D REALLY BE BETTER WITH FROSTING, BUT...WANT SOME?
YES!
THIS IS SO UNEXPECTED COMING FROM YOU!! NO FAIR!
TASTYYY! SO LIGHT AND FLUFFY!
NOM NOM
THIS BLOWS SERO'S SURPRISE RIGHT OUT OF THE WATER.
WHAT A CHARMING HOBBY YOU HAVE, SATO!
WE'LL HAVE TO GET TOGETHER TO COMBINE YOUR CONFECTIONS WITH MY TEA!!
I WASN'T READY FOR THIS REACTION... I ONLY MAKE THESE THINGS TO HELP TRAIN MY QUIRK.
*NOTE: BECAUSE OF SATO'S QUIRK, HE GETS A BOOST WHENEVER HE EATS SUGAR!
DARN... GUESS WE SHOULD'VE EXPECTED SOMETHING TASTY FROM SOMEONE CALLED *SUGARMAN*.
WHAT TIMING, THOUGH... YUM...
CHOMP
CHOMP
THAT'S IT FOR THE BOYS... YUM!
NEXT UP IS... *YUM*... US!
CHEW
CHEW
I COULD GO ALL NIGHT NOW. THAT SUGAR WOKE ME RIGHT UP.
YEAH!
WE HAVE TO HEAD DOWN TO THE FIRST FLOOR TO GET TO THE GIRLS' WING.
*YUM*... SO LET'S GO DOWNSTAIRS...
DO WE HAVE TO? *YUM*...
GAB GAB

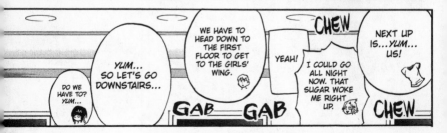

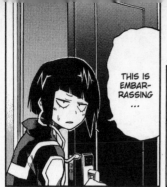

WE'RE REALLY SEEING *EVERYONE'S* ROOM...? IS THAT OKAY?
SHOULD BE OKAY. PROBABLY.
THIS IS EMBARRASSING...
JIRO'S ROOM
THERE'RE EVEN MORE INSTRUMENTS THAN WE THOUGHT!
RIFF
YOU'RE ONE ROCKIN' GIRL, JIRO!
CAN YOU REALLY PLAY ALL THESE?
SOME-WHAT, YEAH...
NOTHING GIRLIE ABOUT THIS ROOM. NOPE.
NON, MADEMOISELLE. ☆
THIS IS IT!
MOVING ON. NEXT!!
NEXT IS ME, HAGAKURE!
BOING
BOING

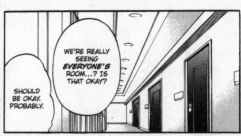

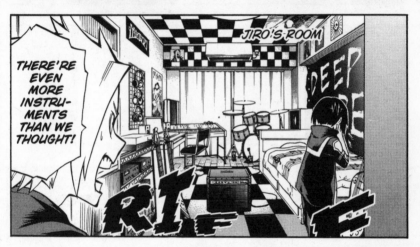

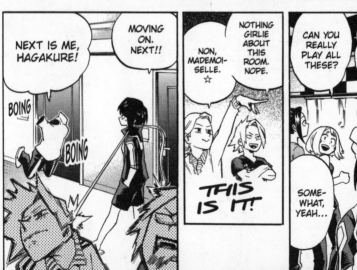

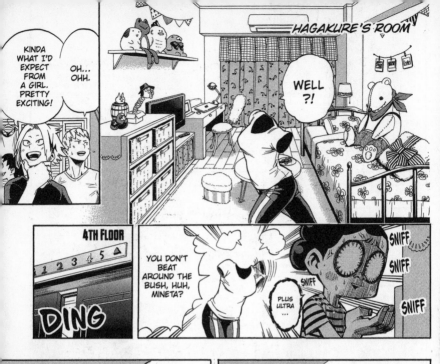

HAGAKURE'S ROOM
WELL ?!
OH... OHH.
KINDA WHAT I'D EXPECT FROM A GIRL. PRETTY EXCITING!
SNIFF
SNIFF
SNIFF
SNIFF
PLUS ULTRA ...
YOU DON'T BEAT AROUND THE BUSH, HUH, MINETA?
4TH FLOOR
1 2 3 4 5
DING
ASHIDO'S ROOM
TA-DAH!! PRETTY CUTE, RIGHT?!
OOH...
URARAKA'S ROOM
WELCOME TO MY BORING ROOM...
OOH ...!

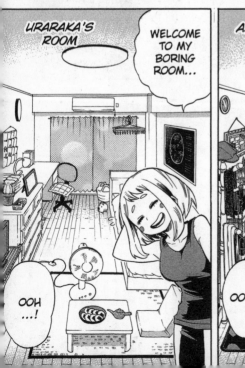

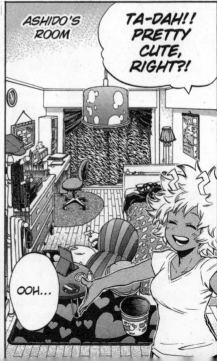

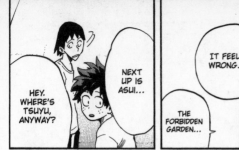

WALKING AROUND AND SEEING ALL THESE GIRLS' ROOMS LIKE IT'S NO BIG DEAL...
IT FEELS WRONG...
THE FORBIDDEN GARDEN...
NEXT UP IS ASUI...
HEY. WHERE'S TSUYU, ANYWAY?
OH, I THINK TSUYU WASN'T FEELING WELL.
NO REASON TO BOTHER HER, THEN.
WE'LL CHECK OUT HER ROOM ANOTHER TIME.
KLIK
LAST UP IS YAOYOROZU!!
BEFORE WE GO IN... LET ME SAY THAT I MISCALCU-LATED...
COMPARED TO ALL YOUR ROOMS, WHICH ARE ALL SO UNIQUE AND ORIGINAL...

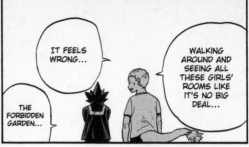

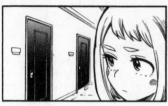

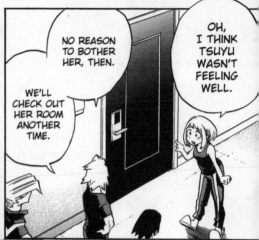

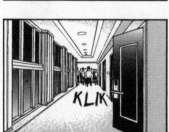

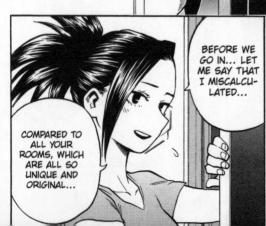

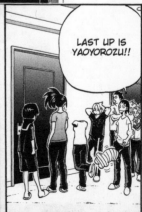

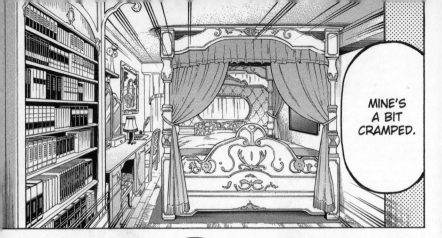

MINE'S A BIT CRAMPED.
HUGE!! BUT CRAMPED!! WHAT HAPPENED, YAOYOROZU?
THIS IS THE SAME STUFF I USE BACK HOME, BUT...
...I NEVER EXPECTED OUR ROOMS HERE WOULD BE QUITE SO SMALL.
WHAT A PRINCESS!
1ST FLOOR
COMMON AREA
OKAY...
HAS EVERYONE FINISHED VOTING?!
REMEMBER, DON'T VOTE FOR YOURSELF!
WITH BAKUGO AND TSUYU OUT OF THE RUNNING...
THE PROVISIONAL FIRST-EVER KING OF ROOMS IS...
THRUST
IS ...!!

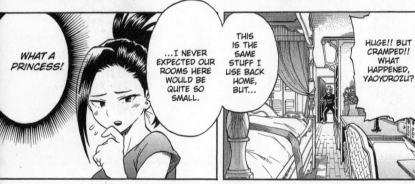

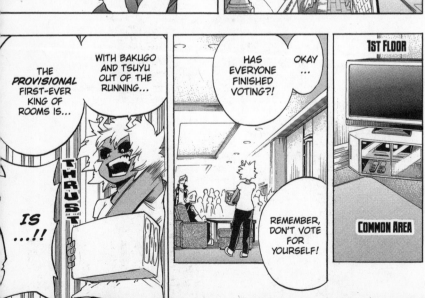

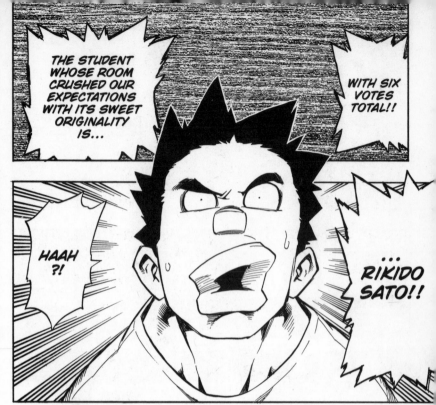

THE STUDENT WHOSE ROOM CRUSHED OUR EXPECTATIONS WITH ITS SWEET ORIGINALITY IS...
WITH SIX VOTES TOTAL!!
... RIKIDO SATO!!
HAAH ?!
BY THE WAY, YOU GOT EVERY SINGLE GIRL'S VOTE!
THE MAIN REASON... THAT YUMMY CAKE!
WHAT ABOUT THE ROOM ?!
NO DECENT WOULD-BE HERO BRIBES PEOPLE!!
HAH HAH HAH
WHAT'RE YOU TALKING ABOUT? I'M JUST HONORED.
ARE WE DONE HERE? CAN I GO TO BED NOW?
NO! YOU MUSTN'T FORGET TO BRUSH YOUR TEETH FIRST, AFTER EATING THAT CAKE!
Ha ha ha.
Stop laughing!!
GUESS WE SHOULD WAIT UNTIL IT'S ALL OVER.

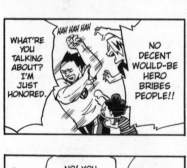

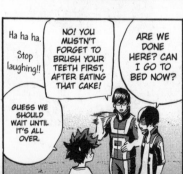

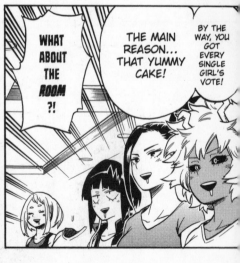

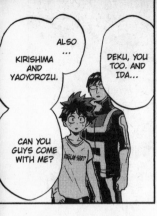

AH! TODO-ROKI.
HOLD ON!
DEKU, YOU TOO. AND IDA...
ALSO ... KIRISHIMA AND YAOYOROZU.
CAN YOU GUYS COME WITH ME?
RAGLAN SHIRT
SO...
TSUYU HAS SOMETHING TO SAY TO YOU ALL.
I USUALLY DON'T HOLD MY TONGUE...

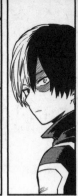

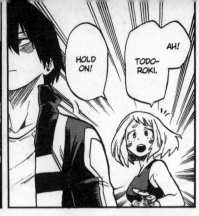

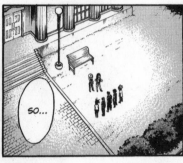

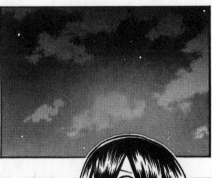

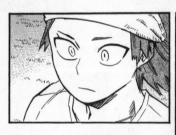

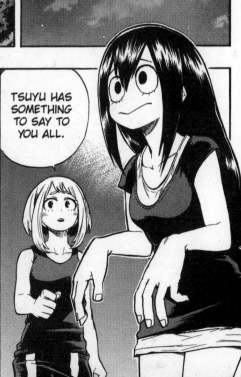

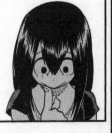

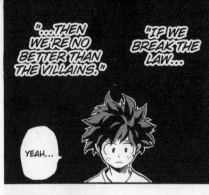

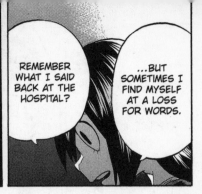

REMEMBER WHAT I SAID BACK AT THE HOSPITAL?
...BUT SOMETIMES I FIND MYSELF AT A LOSS FOR WORDS.
"IF WE BREAK THE LAW...
"...THEN WE'RE NO BETTER THAN THE VILLAINS."
YEAH...
I DIDN'T HOLD BACK.
AND THE WAY I SAID IT WAS KINDA HARSH.
TSUYU ...
SO WHEN I HEARD THIS MORNING THAT YOU GUYS WENT ANYWAY...
I WAS REALLY SHOCKED.
SHOCKED ABOUT HOW I TRIED TO STOP YOU. ABOUT HOW WORTHLESS I AM.
ALL THESE NASTY FEELINGS STARTED TO WELL UP IN ME...
I SUDDENLY HAD NO IDEA WHAT TO SAY.
LIKE THERE WAS NO WAY I COULD GO ON, CHATTING AS IF NOTHING HAD HAPPENED.

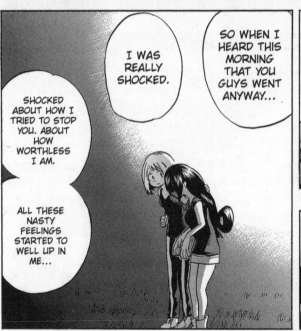

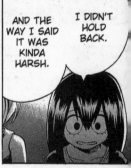

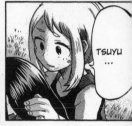

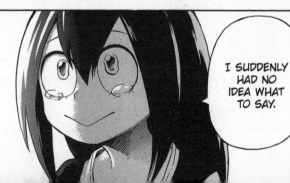

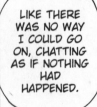

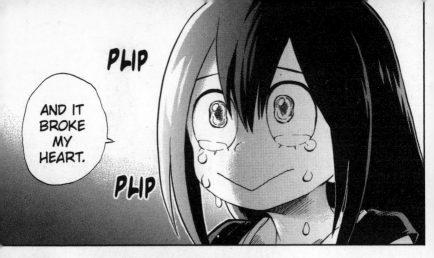

PLIP
AND IT BROKE MY HEART.
PLIP
SO NOW... EVEN IF I'M STILL NOT SURE ABOUT EVERYTHING, I HAD TO SAY SOMETHING...
Raglan T-Shirt
...BECAUSE I WANT TO BE ABLE TO HANG OUT WITH EVERYONE AGAIN.
...
Ribbit Ribbit
IT'S NOT JUST YOU, TSUYU.
WE WERE ALL SUPER UNEASY ABOUT IT.
AND WE ALL WANT TO START OVER AGAIN.
THAT'S WHY...

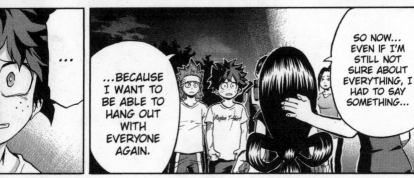

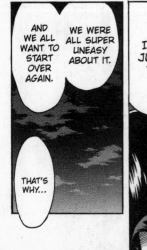

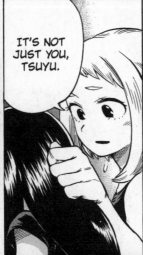

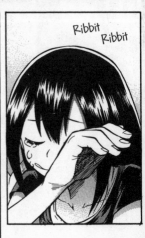

THAT'S WHY WE DO STUFF LIKE THE KING OF ROOMS.
BECAUSE WE KNOW HOW EVERYONE'S FEELING...
WE'RE NOT GONNA GET MAD OR ANYTHING... WE JUST WANT... THIS IS HARD TO EXPLAIN... BUT...
Raglan Shirt
WE WANNA GO BACK TO WHEN...
SHP
...WE COULD ALL JUST SMILE TOGETHER!!
TSUYU ...
I'M SO SORRY !!
THANKS FOR OPENING UP!
ZOOSH
ASUI!
ASU... I MEAN...
TSUYU!
ASU... TSUYU!
RIBBIT!

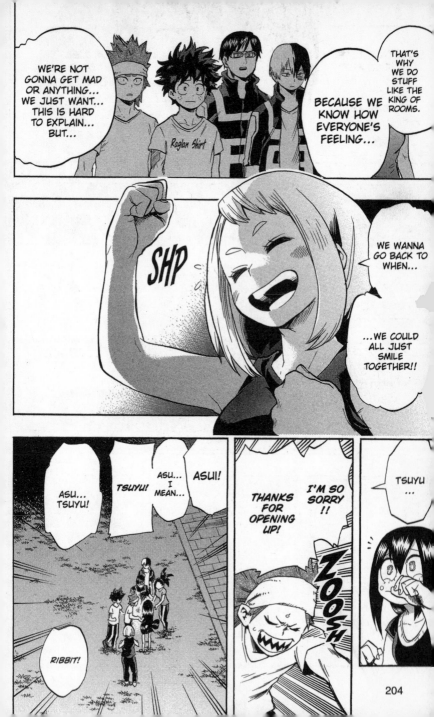

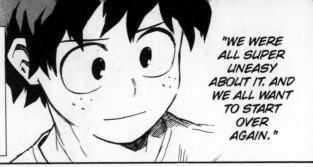

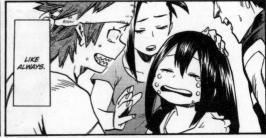

"WE WERE ALL SUPER UNEASY ABOUT IT. AND WE ALL WANT TO START OVER AGAIN."
EVERYONE HAD WORKED SO HARD TO GET THINGS BACK TO HOW THEY WERE BEFORE.
LIKE ALWAYS.
YES. LIKE ALWAYS.
AIMING TO BE HEROES.
PUSHING EACH OTHER TO SUCCEED...
...IN OUR EVERY-DAY LIVES!!

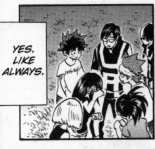

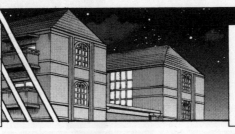

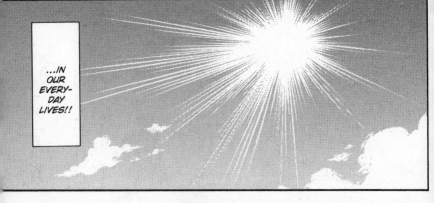

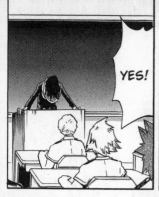

AS I MENTIONED YESTERDAY...
OUR PRIMARY GOAL NOW IS TO GET YOU YOUR PROVISIONAL LICENSES.
YES!
HERO LICENSES ARE INEXTRICABLY TIED TO THE SAVING OF LIVES, SO ONE MUST BE PROPERLY QUALIFIED FOR SUCH A HEAVY RESPONSIBILITY.
NATURALLY, THE TEST IS INCREDIBLY DIFFICULT.
EVEN FOR PROVISIONAL LICENSES, ON AVERAGE WE ONLY SEE A 50 PERCENT SUCCESS RATE.
EVEN THE PROVISIONAL ONE'S THAT HARD TO GET?
FLIK
THAT'S WHY, STARTING TODAY, EACH OF YOU NEEDS TO COME UP WITH AT LEAST TWO...
SHF

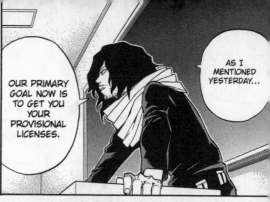

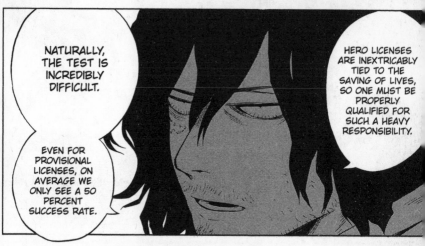

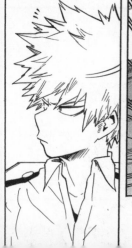

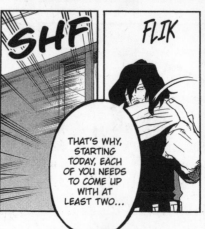

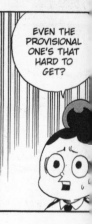

... ULTI-MATE ...
... MOVES !!
THIS IS KINDA LIKE A SCHOOL THING, BUT...
...TOTALLY HERO-LIKE AT THE SAME TIME!!

VOLUME 11 - END OF THE BEGINNING, BEGINNING OF THE END (END)

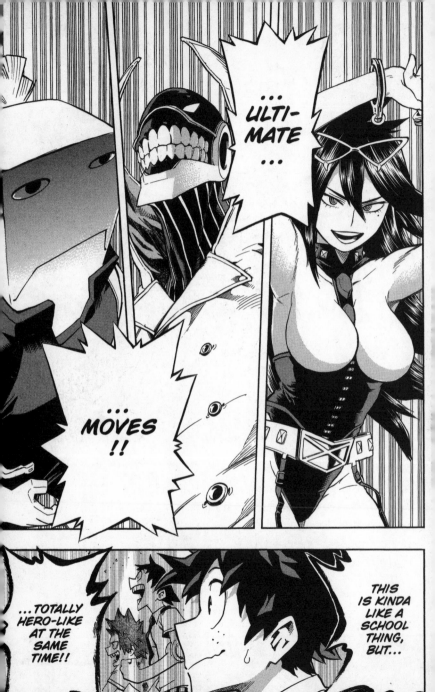

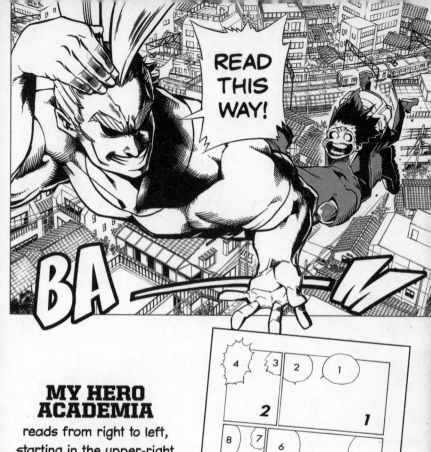

## MY HERO ACADEMIA

reads from right to left, starting in the upper-right corner. Japanese is read from right to left, meaning that action, sound effects and word-balloon order are completely reversed from English order.

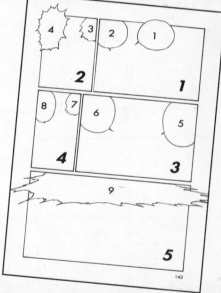